BOURNEMOUTH

The Good Old Days

RODNEY LEGG

HALSGROVE

First published in Great Britain in 2003

Copyright © 2003 Rodney Legg

British Library Cataloguing-in-Publication Data
A CIP record for this title is available from the British Library

ISBN 1 84114 305 7

HALSGROVE
Halsgrove House
Lower Moor Way
Tiverton EX16 6SS
T: 01884 243242
F: 01884 243325

sales@halsgrove.com
www.halsgrove.com

Printed and bound in Great Britain
by CPI Bath Press, Bath

CONTENTS

Dedicated to Victor Loosemore
of Tiverton and Winton Secondary School for Boys

INTRODUCTION

Born in Bournemouth, as was my father a century ago, I am returning to my roots to present this archive of family memories. It centres on the Edwardian heyday that faded away with the Great War. Personal nostalgia for father and then son extends through the devastation of Second World War bombing to the era of post-war austerity and change. In the process I have drawn on my own notebooks and newspaper cuttings dating back to 1960 and will be delighted to receive memories and photographs from readers to add to the collection for future use. I have dozens of files packed with events, dates, people and roads (we were always told that Bournemouth had only one street, which is Orchard Street between Commercial Road and Terrace Road). They are full of both friends and ghosts.

Bournemouth life on the grand and national scale overlaps with the development of suburbs that have grown into the most desirable conurbation in the land. Here I have tried to celebrate it like a latter-day Betjeman – enthusing about piers, railways and trams – though with pictures instead of poems. Antiquarian bookseller John Ruston, my friend for his last two decades, garnished the gossip and introduced me to those he considered significant.

Lillie Langtry and her love-nest with the Prince of Wales in Derby Road start the story. Charles Darwin brought his wife for convalescence on the site of Bournemouth International Centre. Sir Hubert Parry, christened in St Peter's Church, composed 'Jerusalem' without which, it could be argued, there might have been insufficient patriotic fervour to have enabled a First World War to take place. Sir Dan Godfrey brings the background music. Villains include murderers Thomas Allaway and Neville Heath.

The creation of the Undercliff Drive, after the mayoral cutting of the ribbon, was soon followed by breaches from the sea and cliff-falls as nature attempted to reinstate the status quo. The Pier story started the same way, with the original timber framework being replaced in iron by grand master of Victorian pier-building Eugenius Birch. Southbourne's pier was a complete wreck. Boscombe's fared a little better but both it and Bournemouth Pier were reduced to stumps and

islands in 1940 to prevent their use by German invaders. Paddle-steamers returned for their swan-song as similar sounds and smell also disappeared when the railway service into Bournemouth Central ceased, in 1967, to be the last steam-hauled mainline in the land.

Sand artists created tableaux on the beach, ranging from heroes and horses in the Great War through to Biblical scenes in peacetime. Inland, the spectacle of great events included the aviation meeting that claimed the life of Charles Stewart Rolls in 1910, as the first fatality in Britain of powered flight. Crowds filled the Square for carnivals, to glimpse General William Booth of the Salvation Army, and to mark the death of King Edward VII.

Seaside fun gives way at times to events bacteriological and military. Before the world fell apart for the second time in a generation, a medical emergency hit the town, with 51 people dying in the Bournemouth typhoid epidemic of 1936. The town's worst experience in the Second World War was a surprise Sunday lunchtime air raid, in May 1943, killing 77 civilians and a similar number of servicemen. Town centre hotels and shops, plus the bus depot and a church, were left in ruins. These and other buildings destroyed by German raiders remained as bomb-sites for a decade.

The renaissance included the rebuilding of Beales department store and the arrival of Chase Manhattan Bank with its European headquarters. Sir Anthony Eden brought the Conservative Party to the Carlton Hotel in 1955. Bournemouth International Centre has hosted the party conferences of Prime Ministers Thatcher, Major and Blair. This and the targeting of Bournemouth Pier by IRA bombers bring the story into present times.

The biggest 'what might have been' collapsed with the New York stock exchange in 1929. London department store owner Gordon Selfridge had bought Hengistbury Head to build upon it a palatial castle that would be 'the largest house in the world'.

Few great Britons of the past century and a half have not spent time in Bournemouth.

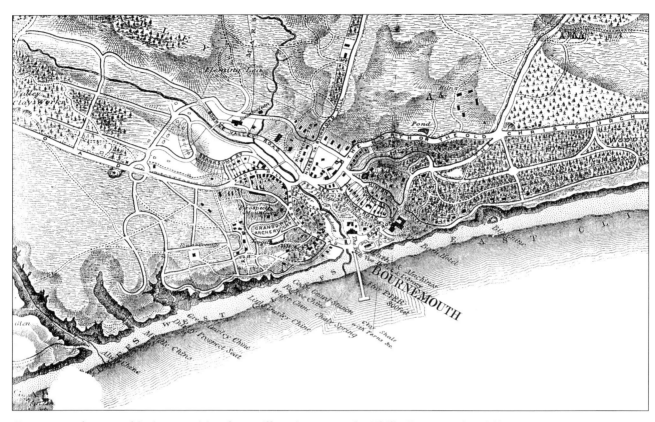

Bournemouth mapped in its transition from village into town, by Philip Brannon, in 1860.

1: NAUGHTY NINETIES

The Red House in Derby Road is now Langtry Manor Hotel. Its foundation stone, dated 1877, carries the initials E.L.L. for Mrs Emilie Le Breton Langtry (1852–1929). Born on Jersey, becoming known as the 'Jersey Lily', she was the most famous and notorious English actress and beauty of the age. Though she had married Edward Langtry in 1874, it was as the mistress of Bertie, Prince of Wales – the future King Edward VII – that she came to Bournemouth. He had the house built and his personal suite of rooms carries the motto *Stet Fortuna Domus* (Let the house stand with good fortune). The lovers entwined their initials on the glass of a downstairs window in 1883 allowing the outside world to enjoy their 'horticultural' joke:

To enjoy a lily properly you need to plant it in a bed.

Just one of Bertie's visits to Bournemouth was an official occasion, on 16 January 1890, when he opened the Royal Victoria Hospital in Poole Road. Bournemouth was the ideal base for visits to Crichel House, the home of Henry Gerard Sturt, 1st Baron Alington (1825–1904) and Lady Augusta Bingham, daughter of the 3rd Earl of Lucan. Lord Alington, who owned 18,000 acres, was Steward of the Jockey Club and a theatre patron. In Crichel Park, the favourite arbour for Bertie and Lillie was the Crow's Nest, a timber turret set in a bridge over a leafy lane.

Lillie Langtry also fell in love with the Prince's nephew, naval officer Prince Louis of Battenburg (1854–1921), and had a daughter by him. Jeanne-Marie Langtry married politician Ian Zachary Malcolm and became Lady Malcolm. Their daughter, Mary Malcolm, was one of the first television announcers. Her grandmother, on meeting Queen Victoria, wore a huge plume of ostrich feathers – the emblem of the Prince of Wales – and the Queen is said to have received Mrs Langtry in silence. The nation, however, remained amused and enthralled, and the friendship with Bertie endured, despite his marriage to Princess Alexandra and their eventual status as King and Queen.

On the hall wall in the Red House, Lillie wrote:

They say – What say they? Let them say.

On the other side of the town, had they known the scandal, they would have been saying things about French poet Paul Verlaine (1844–96). He arrived as an outcast in Bournemouth in 1876, taking rooms at No. 2 Westburn Terrace, at the eastern end of Poole Road, and taught his native tongue and the classics to the boys of Saint Aloysius College. The building survives at what is now No. 24 Surrey Road, on the southwest corner at the crossroads with Queen's Road, in multiple occupation as flats.

Verlaine was managing to stay ahead of his notoriety. He was at the centre of a homosexual scandal which began when he walked out on his wife after eighteen months of marriage and set up home with sixteen-year-old fledgling poet Arthur Rimbaud, ten years his junior, in 1871. Passions ran high and when Rimbaud decided to leave him, Verlaine shot him in the wrist. Released after serving two years' hard labour, Verlaine in 1874 published his *Romances sans paroles,* written in Mons Prison, which borrowed the title of three piano pieces by Fauré.

Verlaine, however, seems to have been blameless in Bournemouth. If anything, the boys tormented their young master, behaving as 'young devils' and knocking him unconscious with a stone concealed in a snowball. Just before returning to his native France, he turned to the scenery for inspiration in the old-fashioned English weather of 1877. The seaside was none too mild that year.

In 'Bournemouth' and 'Le Mer de Bournemouth' the poet describes the paths that pass through tall pines and lead down to the beach:

Le long bois de sapins se tord jusq'au rivage. [The tall pine trees entwine on the shore.]
Le bois sombre descend d'un plateau de bruyere, va dans creuse un vallen, puis monte vert at noir et redescend en fins bosquets. [The dark woods run down from a plateau of heather, going into a hollow ravine, then climb green and black and run down again into sparse thickets.]

The pen picture offers the sound of waves lapping on the beach and then subsumed by pealing church bells on a Sunday morning. As the sun sets seawards there is a church tower looming on land. This was the tower of St Peter's, mother church of the new town, in Gervis Place. It was built by Gothic revival architect George Edmund Street over more than two decades, from initial plans in 1853 when the town's population had just topped 700, with the chancel being completed in 1863 and the tower in 1870. The church and tower were separate entities until the roofing of the vestibules in December 1874. By then the population had reached 6000.

When Paul Verlaine knew St Peter's, it was still incomplete, as it would not be topped off with a spire until 1879. That dominated the Bournemouth skyline, as it rose to 202 feet, which was chosen as being half the height of the spire of Salisbury Cathedral. Saintly statues at each corner of the tower were carved by Thomas Earp. The cross and weathercock on top of the spire were soon blown down, in 1880, and the present cross replaced them in 1882, minus the cock. A tiny brook trickled from a pond on the site of former brickworks in Lorne Park Road, down through Church Glen which was crossed by a rustic bridge, and joined the Bourne Stream in the meadows. Bournemouth, to Verlaine, was still a village though its population had reached 17,000. Homesick, he returned to Paris later in 1877, to continuing notoriety.

Bournemouth, emerging from the pines as a Victorian new town, set a commendable example of how to design a garden city. Meyrick Park is to Bournemouth what Central Park is to New York. Providing the town with the equivalent of a huge village green was achieved by the Commons Preservation Society, having successfully resisted the efforts of the London and South Western Railway Company in 1882–83 to push their line through it with a proposal 'which would have completely bisected the common at its prettiest spot, without leaving a single means of communication from one side to the other'.

The society visualised that Poor's Common – as it was known – promised 'at no very distant time, to become an open space in the midst of a large town' and helped the Bournemouth Improvement Commissioners in petitioning against a Parliamentary bill with the result that 'eventually a deviation of the line, as first suggested by the society, was adopted'.

Here, on the north side, it clips the pine woods 'in the least objectionable manner'. The society also persuaded the lord of the manor, Sir George Meyrick, 'to convey the whole of his interest in the common to the Improvement Commissioners, in order that they may preserve it as a place of recreation'. Meyrick Park covers 194 acres, a third of which was laid out as nearly 4 miles of golf links by Tom Dunn in 1894.

Preservation of what became described as 'the parklands' was enshrined in the Bournemouth Parklands Act of 1889, requiring they 'should be maintained for ever open, unenclosed and unbuilt upon … as open spaces for the recreation and enjoyment of the public'. This legal protection was carried forward into the Bournemouth Corporation Act in 1900, which calls for 'the natural aspect and state of the commons' to be preserved.

J.H. Taylor constructed an 18-hole golf course around the 173 acres of Queen's Park. The smaller King's Park, of 58 acres towards Boscombe, was largely devoted to formal sports. In all, the green lungs of the town's open spaces have expanded to cover some 1500 acres and now comprise a fifth of the area of the borough.

Even Winton, westwards from Wimborne Road, had extensive pine woods but these were generally clear-felled. There are exceptions, such as the cluster of back-garden pines behind the appropriately named Woodend Road, survivors of the great pre-town plantation. 'Winton is neither country nor town,' it was observed in the 1890 parish magazine:

Trees are not favourable to the growth of vegetables, and so far the picturesque is sacrificed to the useful. Much of this wild natural beauty has already succumbed. But attractive as are gorse and heather for the lover of the picturesque, beautiful as are the glimpses of the Stour valley with Ramsdown and St Catherine's Hills beyond the northeastern slopes of Moordown and Charminster, and graceful as is the shade of the West Winton pines in the summer and their shelter in winter, it must be confirmed that Winton's unique attraction consists not in these natural beauties which have their counterparts elsewhere, but in the admirable style, dispositions and arrangements of the working people's houses, especially in the newer parts of the settlement.

Westwards and eastwards the pines have fared better, across Talbot Woods, and on hillocks between the golfing fairways of Queen's Park. The town's other ribbon of open space, narrow and neat but also linear and long, follows the Bourne Stream from source to sea.

Beyond what was then the Boundary Lane, between Hampshire and Dorset, is the 'arcadia in suburbia' of Talbot Village. This was created by philanthropist Miss Georgina Charlotte Talbot between 1850 and 1862. It is notable for its delicate L-shaped cottages, each set in an acre of smallholding, and delightful for their central green and pine woods. The project started as a self-help scheme, an agricultural version of Robert Owen's model industrial community at New Lanark in Scotland.

Two square miles of surrounding fields and woods were bequeathed by Marianne Talbot, Georgina's surviving sister, to Ronald Ruthven Leslie-Melville, 11th Earl of Leven and 10th Earl of Melville (1835–1906), who married the Honourable Emma Selina Portman, eldest daughter of the 2nd Viscount Portman of Bryanston House. The land was destined to become the relatively desirable Talbot Park housing estate and the distinctly up-market Talbot Woods residential area which is clustered around Glenferness Avenue.

Leslie-Melville, one time director of the Bank of England, was director of the Peninsula & Oriental Steamship Company. In 1890, as his memorial to Marianne Talbot, he built Talbot Manor as a home for 'destitute boys'. It was run by the Society for Waifs and Strays which became the Church of England Children's Society. Talbot Manor survives, on the south side of what is now the central roundabout between Talbot Avenue and Wallisdown Road. Tucked into the hedge beside it is a pre-Bournemouth boundary stone, cut with 'Parish of Holdenhurst' on the east side and 'County of Dorset' facing west.

Down on the beach, the 'fashionable watering place' of Sandbourne, as it was named by Thomas Hardy in *Tess of the d'Urbervilles*, had strict bye-laws. Mixed bathing was allowed in places but in the vicinity of segregated bathing machines it was forbidden to swim within 20 yards of areas reserved for the opposite sex. Female bathers were obliged to wear 'a tunic, or blouse, reaching from the neck to the knee, with belt and knickerbocker drawers'.

Bournemouth competed with the Isle of Wight in appealing to invalids. The 'peculiar sedative influence of its climate' was attributed by its Medical Officer of Health to a combination of pure air and the exhalation of its plentiful pines 'giving off into the atmosphere a terebinthine oxygenating influence'. A wide, flat terrace beneath the trees, between Westover Road and the Lower Central Gardens, was designated as Invalids' Walk, with ample room for their Bath chairs.

The Scots pines, originally a forest of an estimated three million trees, were planted by landowner Sir George Tapps at the turn of the nineteenth century. In 1835 they were inherited by Sir George William Tapps-Gervis who commissioned Christchurch architect Benjamin Ferrey to create 'the new marine village of Bourne'. By 1836 they had completed 16 villas along the north side of Westover Road, with a view over the stream to the sea. Then, as now, developers and administrators conspired to construct obstacles to block that wonderful view. First were the Bath Hotel and Belle Vue Hotel, though the immediate stream-side was preserved as pleasure gardens. The Bath Hotel – the town's first – was another Gervis-Ferrey creation. It opened on one of the century's great dates, Queen Victoria's coronation day, on 28 June 1838. Its sweeping white façade, embellished with corner turrets but otherwise unostentatious, soon saw the arrival of hosts of notables. Its first monarch-to-be, appropriately in the light of future associations, was Prince Bertie at age fifteen, visiting incognito with two aides on a walking tour, in September 1856.

Prime Minister Benjamin Disraeli was sent here by Queen Victoria and his doctors, for relief from the gout and to avoid the worst of the cold winter of 1874–75. Even in Bournemouth's premier hotel he found it impossible to keep his room temperatures in the 60s Fahrenheit. That must have been sorted as the Royal Bath Hotel won its five stars upon introduction of the grading system in 1912.

Upstream from the Square, the Monte Dore Hotel – now the Town Hall – opened as a centre for hydrotherapy. It was launched in splendid style, by King Oscar I of Scandinavia in 1855, and marked Bournemouth's emergence as a seaside spa. Medical attention for the ailing rich was provided in the adjoining Royal National Sanatorium for Consumption and Diseases of the Chest. In three acres of grounds, above Bourne Avenue, this was designed by Sir Arthur Blomfield in 1855. The most famous of its Victorian sufferers, briefly retiring to Skerryvore at No. 61 Alum Chine Road, Westbourne, was Robert Louis Stevenson (1850–94) of *Treasure Island* fame. During his time in Bournemouth, before moving on to New York and Samoa, he wrote *Kidnapped* and *The Strange Tale of Dr Jekyll and Mr Hyde*.

The American novelist Henry James (1843–1916), who moved from New York to London in 1876, stayed in Bournemouth in 1885, from 18 April until 30 June. He lodged at St Alban's in Southcliff Road and was completing *The Bostonians* when he visited Robert Louis Stevenson in Skerryvore. He dismissed Stevenson as a 'shirt-collarless Bohemian poseur' and the compliment was reciprocated by RLS writing a poem in which James features as a 'bland colossus'.

Henry James was not easily pleased. He saw in Victorian Bournemouth the urbanised sameness that Norman Mailer would denounce as 'airport modern' a century later. 'Bournemouth,' James thundered, 'has an almost American newness and ugliness.' Its single saving grace was the view across to the Isle of Wight, looking like 'a pretty marble toy on an ultramarine horizon'.

Mrs Fanny Stevenson got on much better with James and delighted in his company, smoothing the literary relationship and encouraging his return to Bournemouth the following year, in February 1886. RLS then writes of James's gift to them of a 'magic mirror' from Venice in which they visualise the reflection of the kindly face 'of a friend entwined' and elevates him in purple prose … 'the Prince of men, Henry James shall come again'.

James did return after Stevenson's departure and death, with his typist Miss McAlpine, to the Royal Bath Hotel in 1897.

Development on the east side of the Square, overlooking what were then paddocks and meadow, began with the four-storey shops and apartments of Southbourne Terrace, on the north side of Old Christchurch Road. There were six wide-fronted modern shops, with accommodation above, built by Henry Joy in 1863. On the west side, St Andrew's Presbyterian Church, timber-built in 1857, was rebuilt in stone in 1872. This also proved too small and the congregation moved to Exeter Road in 1887, into a huge new building with a spire 140-feet high.

Big and brash buildings were springing up everywhere. Punshon Memorial Methodist Church, on the east side of Richmond Hill, opened in June 1866.

The 60-bed Herbert Convalescent Home, in Alumhurst Road, opened in 1867 as a memorial to Lord Herbert of Lea who died in 1861. Holy Trinity Church, on the east side of Horseshoe Common, was built in 'diapered red brick, in the Lombardo-Gothic style' in 1869, with a matching 112-feet tower being added in 1877.

St Clement's Church in Knole Road was built in 1872. The Catholic Oratory of the Sacred Heart on Richmond Hill, with its 80-feet tower and Angelus bell, dates from 1875 and was enlarged in 1898. The Baptist Church in Lansdowne Road was built in 1876. So too was St Michael's and All Angels though its tower was added in 1901. St Swithun's Church, Gervis Road East, was built between 1876 and 1891.

In 1872, Revd W.W. Herringham bought land for a church, vicarage and school on the west side of Wimborne Road at Moordown. The Earl of Malmesbury laid the foundation stone for the church of St John the Baptist on 6 August 1873 and the Bishop of Winchester, Dr Harold Browne, consecrated the building on 14 April 1874. A school for girls and infants followed in 1877, with the Church of England Boys' Day School being built later, on the corner of Bemister Road and Luther Road, in 1892. Curates from St John's had a reputation for boxing with the boys in the gymnasium and one, at least, appeared at Sunday services 'sporting a splendid black eye'.

The Catholic benefactor Lady Georgiana Fullerton, for whom Bournemouth was 'full of sorrows and sad destinies', founded the Convent and Convalescent Home of St Joseph, Branksome Wood Road, in 1874.

The 32-bed Hahnemann Convalescent Home, on the West Cliff, dated from 1879. St Paul's Church, overlooking the Central Station, dated from 1881 to 1887 and had its spire erected in 1903 as a memorial to Queen Victoria. St Stephen's Church beside Gordon Grove – now St Stephen's Road, between Richmond Hill and the Town Hall – was built between 1881 and 1897 in memory of Revd Alexander Morden Bennett who was the founder and first vicar of St Peter's Church.

Nos 5 and 6 Richmond Hill became Stewart's Private Hotel. Its first famous visitors, 'over-wintering in Bournemouth' were the Duke and Duchess of Norfolk, as a result of which it became the Norfolk Hotel. The Imperial Hotel opened beside the Square in 1887. Lansdowne House – in the triangular junction of Holdenhurst Road and Christchurch Road – was replaced by the Metropole Hotel in 1890.

The church of St John the Evangelist in Surrey Road was built in 1889. Its tower was completed in 1906. Revd Edward Cleal, a Fabian socialist, became minister of Winton Congregational Church, on Peters Hill, in 1890. By coincidence, his mentor Sidney Webb was convalescing at the Osborne, a boarding house opposite the Royal Exeter Hotel on the southern corner of Priory Road and Exeter Road. As well as establishing a penny bank, library and cricket club for working-class Winton, Cleal formed its Band of Hope, to challenge the influence of a beer seller next door. Cleal and George Underwood, a picture framer at No. 88a Commercial Road, founded Bournemouth Fabian Society on 13 November 1892.

The society nevere had more than 15 members but they included Miss Beatrice Potter (1858–1943), from Kildare on Bath Hill, who enrolled in the spring of 1893. She had impeccable capitalist roots, as the eighth daughter of Richard Potter, former chairman of the Great Western Railway and president of the Grand Trunk Railway of Canada. Beatrice, as Mrs Sidney Webb, became the conscience of the twentieth-century Labour Party.

East Cliff Congregational Church was built in 1891 when the town's population reached 37,650. St Augustin's Church, at the Cemetery Junction, was also built in 1891. The crossroads above a wide railway bridge took its name from the 25 acres of cemetery, with a drive flanked by an avenue of monkey-puzzle trees, a mile to the north of the town centre. Its mortuary chapel, designed by Christopher Crabbe Creeke, had half its area consecrated according to Anglican rites, with the remainder 'apportioned to the Nonconformists'.

St Andrew's Church in Bennett Road was built between 1891 and 1900. St Mary the Virgin was dedicated in 1895 and rebuilt in 1927. The foundation stone of St Luke's Church in Winton was laid on Ascension Day in 1897 and it was eventually completed and dedicated on St Luke's Day in 1913. Most of these churches had their halls and schools. There was also a Shaftesbury Hall, in St Peter's Road, owned by the Young Men's Christian Association. Cairns Memorial House, the Digby Institute and Havergal Hall provided other

YMCA venues. The Theatre Royal in Albert Road, managed by Harry Nash, was enlarged and reopened as Bournemouth Theatre and Opera House in 1892.

Thomas James Hankinson, guidebook publisher and estate agent, became Bournemouth's first Mayor in 1890. A member of the board of Bournemouth Improvement Commissioners since 1873, he established the Victoria Library beside Victoria House in the Exeter Road approach to the Square. Hankinson's businesses moved to Richmond Chambers, at the bottom of Richmond Hill, in 1875. The 17-strong Board of Improvement Commissioners were incorporated by royal charter, as a municipal borough council, in 1890. The charter was sent to the town by rail, from the Privy Council, on 27 August 1890 and then taken by coach to the Pier Approach where it was read to a huge crowd by the secretary to the commissioners, James Druitt. Bournemouth remained part of the Hampshire parishes of Christchurch and Holdenhurst for a little longer, until being created as a parish in its own name, by the Local Government Act, 1894.

The Wessex writer Clive Holland (1866–1958), born Charles James Hankinson, was the Mayor's eldest son. Clive became a close friend of Thomas Hardy, cycling with him and then driving him in advancing age, around the Dorset heights to picnic at viewpoints featured in the famous novels. This enabled Holland to write for American and British journals but for all the closeness of literary association the words are disappointingly bland.

Far more interesting, Marguerite Radclyffe Hall (1886–1943) was born at No. 6 Durley Road, on the south side of Poole Hill. Her poems and novels were a triumph. *Adam's Breed* in 1926 took the James Tait-Black Prize and was followed by *The Well of Loneliness* in 1928. As a study of lesbianism, it proved too hot for London publishers to handle and its first edition appeared in the United States. Radclyffe Hall moved on from Bournemouth and is buried in Highgate Cemetery.

From 1876 to 1881, Saugeen Preparatory School in Derby Road had its most notable literary pupil, the author and playwright John Galsworthy (1867–1933), though he was being groomed for Harrow and Oxford, where he studied law. *Jocelyn*, published in 1898, set him off on an alternative career. He went on to create *The Forsyte Saga* in 1922. In 1929 he replaced Thomas Hardy as the writing member of the Order of Merit and went one better by taking the Nobel Prize for literature in 1932.

Music in Bournemouth started with a 16-strong Italian Band in 1876. The ex-soldiers, still wearing their Italian military uniforms, migrated to the English seaside from Bath. The remaining Italians and Bournemouth's first Town Band were brought together for the summer of 1892 as the Corporation Military Band, with 21 players, under the direction of Signor E. Bertini. Concerts took place twice a day on Bournemouth Pier.

These came indoors, into the glass-roofed Winter Gardens, on Whit Monday in 1893. Southbourne authoress Jesse Bedford described it as 'a concert hall in the style of a huge cucumber frame, especially adapted to the requirements of invalids and ferns'. The 30 performers in what was now Dan Godfrey's Military Band wore dark-blue uniforms with gold facings. Initially, they continued with their tunes but the first 'classical and symphony concert' took place on 14 October 1895. It was conducted by Godfrey, with Walter J. Evans, as leader of the orchestra. They had become the Bournemouth Municipal Orchestra.

Sir Dan Godfrey (1868-1939) lived at St Margaret's in Priory Road and then Dannholme in Alumhurst Road. Even after his knighthood, in 1922, he could only claim to be Bournemouth's second great musician. Ahead of him, in terms of both local and national fame, was Sir Hubert Parry (1848–1919), composer of 'Jerusalem' and 'Blest Pair of Sirens', who was born in Bournemouth and christened at St Peter's Church in Hinton Road. He first conducted his own work in the Winter Gardens on 1 March 1900 and was commemorated with a plaque:

A great musician whose influence on British music will always be remembered.

About this time the town had the excitement of a murder. On the morning of Tuesday 27 February 1894 William Wilkins, foreman of the omnibus company, was fatally wounded at the stables in Pokesdown. He died later at home, with Dr Dickie thinking he had been kicked by a horse, until 'a round metal object' was found embedded in his skull. The chief suspect, as the last person to see him at work, was chaff-cutter and traction engine driver Samuel Elkins (also called Tom), sacked the previous weekend for bullying the stable-lads. He had taken a train to Southampton to buy a revolver.

Elkins went to Boscombe to find a policeman, asked him to come for a drink but found he was teetotal, and then insisted on being arrested. Only after he produced the gun was Sergeant Robin Hood – that was his name – persuaded that there might be something to his confession:

I up with the revolver and fired it off and he dropped down dead.

Elkins went on trial for murder at Winchester in June 1894. He refused to present any defence and insisted on pleading guilty, telling Lord Justice Lawrence that he realised the implications:

Yes, pass the sentence of death my lord.

The judge showed more emotion than the accused as he did so, to conclude one of the shortest capital trials in post-medieval British legal history. It had lasted eight minutes. There was no last-minute expression of remorse when Samuel Elkins, displaying the same confidence, went to the gallows on 18 July 1894.

The other prominent Bournemouth name of 1894 was that of insurance underwriter Merton Russell Cotes (1835–1921) who had retired to the town on buying the Bath Hotel in 1876. He proceeded to take an active part in developing the town and donated its mace – a replica of that presented to Wolverhampton by Queen Elizabeth I – in 1890. Ill-health prevented him taking up the offer of the mayoral chair in 1892 and 1893. Then, in 1894, he accepted and was in office for the opening of Meyrick Park, two public libraries, and two schools of art.

On the hill above the Bath Hotel, up what is now Russell Cotes Road, he built East Cliff Hall – which 'from the foreshore looks like a collection of salt and pepper-pots' – to mark the conclusion of his year as Mayor in 1895. There he entertained the actor Sir Henry Irving (1838–1905) and proceeded to fill the building with an eclectic mix of Victoriana and eastern *objets d'art*. Home and contents were given to the town in 1908, after it had acceded to his demands for an Undercliff Drive, and are now the Russell-Cotes Museum. The following year Merton Russell Cotes was knighted.

Boscombe could claim its own seaside symbol from 1889 with the opening by the Duke of Argyll of Boscombe Pier. Southbourne also had its pier, until it was strewn along the beach by a gale, never to be rebuilt.

In 1890 a new Richmond Hill Congregational Church, costing £17,000 and with seating for 1100, replaced the original chapel that had opened for worship on 8 March 1859. During its building the Sunday services were held in the Shaftesbury Hall and evening services in the lecture hall beside the nearby 1886-built Punshon Memorial Wesleyan Church. 'The house is great for great is our God,' was the text chosen by its pastor, Revd J. Ossian Davies, for the opening service of the new Richmond Hill Congregational Church. Davies left for Paddington Chapel, London, in 1898 and was succeeded by Revd Joseph David Jones who remained in post until 1937.

The Central Hotel, towards the bottom of the east side of Richmond Hill, was built in 1886. It and the Central Chambers of 1888, on the site of two Presbyterian churches beside Bourne Avenue, were designed by Bournemouth architects Lawson & Donkin. Beside the Central Hotel, overlooking the Square, the Cadena Cafe and the Mansion Hotel, succeeded by the Empress Hotel, occupied this prime site until after the First World War. Then the National Provincial Bank expanded from its original 1879-built home and acquired the entire corner.

The first 'handsome and adequate' pier on Bournemouth beach was opened on 17 September 1861. Shipworm soon discovered and devoured the timber piles. On 5 January 1867 its weaknesses were tested to destruction by storm-force winds:

High on the beach it was thrown like a stranded wreck on a sandbank; fall piles wrested in twain, and iron twisted like packthread, covered the yellow strand of the sun-loving village of Bournemouth.

Three hundred feet had been lost, along with its toll-house, and another 100 feet was lopped off in a gale in 1876 and washed up at Swanage. The sad remnant was completely rebuilt, after Florence Newlyn laid its foundation stone on 9 November 1878. It had pavilions and promenades, elegant abutments and a bandstand, plus moorings and galleries for servicing the steamers that were catering for the masses who were swarming to the seaside. The cast-iron structure was designed by Eugenius Birch, the grand master of Victorian pier-building, which was very much an English expertise. The main span, 838 feet long and 35 feet wide, expanded into a pier-head, 110 feet wide,

at the seaward end. It opened in 1880. *Pulchritudinas et Salubritas* (Beauty and Health) was adopted as the town's official motto but 'See Bournemouth and die' might have been more appropriate.

The poet and divine John Keble (1792–1866) started that trend. He was the best-known churchman of the age and his hymn-book *The Christian Year* was in its 95th edition by the time he died. Keble moved from Romsey to Brookside, above Pier Approach, in 1865. He died there the following year and the house became part of the White Hermitage Hotel in Exeter Road. 'That was where John Keble died,' I was told half a century ago. Not many people will know that, these days, or even who he was.

Sir Henry Taylor (1801–86), author of the historical novel *Philip van Artevelde*, moved to the Roost – since named Rawden – in Hinton Road, in the 1860s. 'The place is beautiful beyond any seaside place I have ever seen except the Riviera,' he wrote on first sight of the resort in 1861.

Another admirer of the Riviera, Hugh McCalmont Cairns, 1st Earl Cairns (1819–85), was Disraeli's Lord Chancellor. He built a house in Manor Road in 1873. This was called Lindisfarne and he died there on 2 April 1885.

Major-General Richard Clement Moody (1813–87) of the Royal Engineers, founder of New Westminster as capital for the new colony of British Columbia, retired to Lyme Regis. He died from apoplexy while visiting Bournemouth, on 31 March 1887, and is buried at the top of the Thirty-nine Steps in St Peter's churchyard. These predate John Buchan and his character Richard Hannay but were chosen for the same reason – by first vicar Revd Alexander Morden Bennett – signifying the Thirty-nine Articles of Religion of the Church of England.

Art nouveau book illustrator Aubrey Beardsley (1872–98) came to Bournemouth hoping for a respite from his failing health. He was terminally ill with tuberculosis. First he stayed at Pier View Hotel, above Boscombe Chine, in July 1896, and was visited by London publisher Leonard Smithers who commissioned a collection of 50 drawings. By the time he returned to Bournemouth, to stay in Muriel Guest-House in the triangle between Exeter Road and Terrace Road, he could hardly hold a pen. There, on 31 March 1897, he received his first holy communion on entering the Catholic Church.

Former Prime Minister and statesman William Ewart Gladstone (1809–1898) was dying when he stayed at Forest House, in Grove Road, Bournemouth, in 1898. He took his final communion in St Peter's Church and made his last public utterances beneath the clock on the up-platform at the town's Central Station as he left for his home in Wales on 22 March 1898.

Lillie Langtry also moved on, following the dissolution of her marriage in 1897, and married Sir Hugo Gerald de Bathe in 1899. She was now an impresario, directing and acting under her own management in London and New York, before following the sun southwards to Monaco, where she died in 1929. Bournemouth, meanwhile, was continuing to grow,

with a population of 60,000 at the turn of the century. Boscombe St John's Lads' Institute Football Club, formed in 1890, met at No. 60 Gladstone Road in the summer of 1899 and renamed itself Boscombe Football Club. Charlie Hembrey was its first captain, quickly succeeded by Charlie Stevenson, then Ted Kerley. Their home ground was at Castlemain Road, Pokesdown, and selections were discussed under a gas lamp to save on hiring a room. Competing in the 1899–1900 season in the Bournemouth and District Junior League, and for the Hants Junior Cup, the team chose red and white for its colours and became known as 'the Cherries of Boscombe'. In the new century it evolved into Bournemouth and Boscombe Athletic Football Club.

Bournemouth's natural seaside, as represented by Middle Chine, which still looked like this until the turn of the twentieth century.

Some of the last wind-blown specimens of Bournemouth's three million pine trees survived beside 'the favourite walk' on West Cliff.

The archetypal view of Victorian Bournemouth, in one of the earliest photographs of Invalids' Walk, through the Scots pines beside Westover Road, complete with a lady in a Bath chair (centre) with her nurse and a gentleman in top hat.

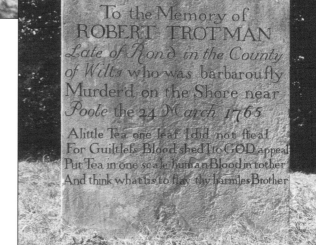

Smuggler's epitaph, in Kinson churchyard, as evidence of the former trade along the holiday coast.

Eighteenth-century Tapps Arms, renamed the Tregonwell Arms, which doubled as Bournemouth's first Post Office from 1839 to 1861.

Lewis Tregonwell's 1810-built cottage, later named Portman Lodge, and St Andrew's Presbyterian Church in Exeter Road.

The Red House in Derby Road, now Langtry Manor Hotel, was built as a love-nest by Edward, Prince of Wales.

Bournemouth beauty Mrs Lillie Langtry, mistress of the Prince of Wales, painted by Sir John Millais.

This 1839-dated watercolour by Celia Montgomery gives us the only known glimpse of ancient Holdenhurst parish church (left), before the Anglo-Saxon building was demolished after consecration of the neo-Gothic replacement (right).

'Parish of Holdenhurst' covered much of Bournemouth, as is proved by this boundary stone at Talbot Manor, between Winton and Wallisdown.

White Farm, in Talbot Woods, where a philanthropic model village embodied Victorian self-help ideals.

Timber (foreground) laid out to be used constructing the first Bournemouth Pier, Belle Vue Hotel (centre left) and Exeter Road (centre right) in 1860.

First Presbyterian Church at the foot of Richmond Hill (left) and Southbourne Terrace beside Old Christchurch Road in the view northwards across the meadows from Exeter Road in 1865.

The Square before it had the name, westwards from Gervis Place (left) and Old Christchurch Road (right) to the bridge over the Bourne Stream (centre) and Commercial Road (centre right).

Pier Approach and the creation of the grand master of Victorian pier-building, Eugenius Birch, which opened in 1880.

The 1880-built second Bournemouth Pier, looking eastwards from the exposed sandy strata of an untamed West Cliff.

Newly completed Bournemouth Pier, showing its cast-iron flourishes, in a view northwestwards to the villas of Southcliff Road (top left).

The day Bournemouth received its identity, with a charter from the Privy Council being read at the Pier Approach by solicitor James Druitt, on 27 August 1890.

By 1890 there was standing room only on Bournemouth beach, as is shown by this view from the pier, northeastwards to East Cliff Hall (top right).

Victorian ladies and gentlemen on Bournemouth Pier in the 1890s, with evidence of orderly society (the sign says 'Please keep to the right').

Boats, shelters beside the beach and villas along Bath Road to the flag-flying Royal Bath Hotel (top right) in a view northeastwards from Bournemouth Pier towards the turn of the century.

Paddle-steamer reversing out from Bournemouth Pier in the 1890s, in a view from East Cliff, which show rows of bathing machines on the beach.

The Square southwards into Exeter Road, from Hugh King's drapery store (with blind) to St Andrew's Presbyterian Church, in the 1890s.

The Lower Gardens in the 1890s, northwestwards across the Square (centre left) to the Town Hall (top left), St Stephen's Church (centre), Richmond Chambers, The Mansion (later Empress Hotel) and spire of Punshon Memorial Church (just visible far right).

Robert Louis Stevenson who completed Kidnapped *and* The Strange Story of Dr Jekyll and Mr Hyde *while living in Westbourne.*

Oriental House, founded by John Elmes Beale in 1881, and the Burlington Arcade (right) in Old Christchurch Road.

The bells of St John's Church at Boscombe in Surrey Road, Bournemouth, was built in 1889 with the bell tower being added in 1906.

Fresh graves beside St John's Church in Moordown.

The classic photograph of Oscar Wilde was taken by Debenham and Gould at their Glen View Studio in Bournemouth, in the early 1890s.

The Royal Arcade (centre) in Christchurch Road, Boscombe, with bootmakers A. Jones & Sons and lofty apartments between the Salisbury Hotel (left) and The Grand (right).

2: EDWARDIAN ERA

The County Borough of Bournemouth came into existence on 1 April 1900 and immediately set about extending its boundaries. By August 1901 its 2593 acres had been more than doubled, to 5850 acres, by incorporating the urban districts of Pokesdown and Winton, the Richmond Park district of Holdenhurst parish, and the eastern parish of Southbourne. The population numbered 69,340.

For Southbourne, however, there was a setback. Its 300-feet pier, built in 1888, was wrecked by double gales on 28 December 1900 and 3 January 1901. It remained derelict until removal of the debris in 1907. The eastern seaboard was also subject to cliff-falls which gradually ate away at gardens and eventually left buildings hanging over the edge.

Weymouth-born department store owner John Elmes Beale (1848–1928), who founded his Fancy Fair at No. 3 St Peter's Terrace in 1881, was the town's Mayor from 1902 to 1905. The other great stores were Brights of Bournemouth and Plummer Roddis in Old Christchurch Road, Bobby's in the Square, and Harvey Nichols in Commercial Road. The expanding town faced a booming future.

For some it was England's equivalent of New York. The exiled Russian Count Vladimir Chertkov (1855-1937) came to Bournemouth in 1897. His mother had a holiday home, Slavanka, at Tuckton. They bought Tuckton House and the Old Waterworks, Saxonbury Road, Southbourne, establishing a printing press to produce essays and plays by Count Leo Nikolayevich Tolstoy (1828–1910), expounding what became Tolstoyism.

Thirty émigrés were working in Southbourne, operating as an organised sect, by the time Chertkov was allowed back to Russia in 1905. The colony gradually dispersed and eventually disbanded in 1913. Chertkov's mother refused to go home, however, and ended her days at Slavanka in 1922. She is buried in Christchurch cemetery.

The tramway system through the Square opened in December 1902 and a line up Richmond Hill was added in 1903 in order to provide a direct route to Winton and Charminster. The *Bournemouth Graphic*

reported that this was almost a hill too far and it remained off limits for descending vehicles:

'This gradient has been a very expensive luxury and is possibly one which will result in a loss of profits for some years to come.'

The tram network was on the move, embracing the whole conurbation from Poole to Christchurch, with the rebuilding of Tuckton Bridge. Its 1882-built timbers were completely replaced by a lattice of thin arches in modern concrete. The first tram crossed the new bridge, from Bournemouth to Christchurch, on 17 October 1905. A side loop of track was added on the south side of the Square, between the outer line and its circle of grass, in 1906.

This layout remained unchanged until 1921. I came to hear much about the era of the tram, authenticated by a photograph of my father which shows him as a conductor for Bournemouth Corporation Tramways, with Driver Frost and two points-men who were key to the operation of the system.

By a remarkable coincidence, this photograph of 1916 was accompanied by an earlier postcard, of a tram coming westwards around the Square. The 'No. 72' was the clue to its significance. This picture can be precisely dated to the summer of 1907. It shows a tramcar which came into service that year but failed to see the next season (or so it was generally thought). Disaster occurred on May Day in 1908, when it came off the rails in Avenue Road, and crashed through the trees to end up 20 feet below in the grounds of Fairlight Glen.

Seven passengers were killed and 26 seriously injured, making it 'the most serious tramways accident in the United Kingdom', as it was described at the subsequent inquiry. The tram had been on its way eastwards to Fisherman's Walk at Southbourne. The magnetic brake failed on Poole Hill. Having jumped the metals, the car left the road, 'its stability not helped by an adverse camber'.

Driver William Wilton was exonerated. Though seriously injured himself he assisted in the rescue work. Transport fitter Harry Upshall, from Bagber at Sturminster Newton, then helped to haul the wreckage back on to the road. He continued working on tramcars until No. 115 took the last service from the Square to Christchurch, on 8 April 1936, and recalled the tragedy when he celebrated his ninety-first birthday. That was in 1966 when I met him in the Blackmore Vale.

After 1908, there was never another Bournemouth tramcar No. 72, but unknown to most of its users the ill-fated tramcar had been repaired and put back into service. 'It was repainted as No. 71,' Harry Upshall revealed.

The transition from Victorian to Edwardian times was marked by the establishment and growth of the Carlton Hotel which was a sea-view house called Brumstath, on the East Cliff, bought by the newly formed Bournemouth & District Property Company in 1900. Four of its eight directors became Mayor of Bournemouth. The house was being leased as a convent, to an order of nuns from Roehampton, when there was a change of direction. The Carlton was launched as 'A First-class Boarding Establishment' after the addition of 40 rooms at a cost of £3600. Electric light and 'meals at separate tables' featured in its advertisements. The reporter from the town's newspaper – the *Bournemouth Graphic* which had its offices in Richmond Chambers on the Bourne Avenue side of the Square – found himself duly impressed:

Inside the Carlton is luxury itself. Entering through a stately portico, a smartly dressed page ushers the visitor into the great hall, where he at once realises the comfort and stateliness of the establishment. Here, guests are enjoying their morning weed [tobacco] and paper, or chatting over the events of the day, comfortably unconcerned in the easiest of chairs and evidently revelling in their surroundings.

The whole of the woodwork is in turned oak, even to the picture frames and general fitments. The hall and lounges are covered with rich Turkey carpets, and there is an abundance of couches, settees and easy chairs, much of the furniture being of Sheraton style with rich coverings of yellow and green silk.

The 'boarding house' expanded from Brumstath to absorb and incorporate the next villa, Broadley, and then into a third, Leeholme, in 1917. After that, as the complex was completed with the addition of an east wing, the Carlton was given a dispensation by the Meyrick Estate, in March 1928, to style itself 'an hotel'. Five-star rating was achieved in 1934.

East Cliff Drive opened in July 1904 and was followed below by the Undercliff Drive – Bournemouth's promenade – which resulted from a long campaign by Merton Russell Cotes and his Undercliff Drive and Pavilion League, against opposition from Bournemouth Residents' Association.

The first section to be completed was from Bournemouth Pier to the ladder and cables on the construction site for the electrically operated East Cliff Lift below Meyrick Road. There the Mayor, J.A. Parsons, cut the ribbon on 6 November 1907. The next extension of the promenade, westwards from the pier to West Cliff Lift, began in 1911. It was also lengthened in the other direction, from East Cliff Lift to Boscombe Pier, where the opening ceremony was performed by the Earl of Malmesbury on 3 June 1914.

Malmesbury Park, named for its former landowner, was expanding fast and had been provided with a Wesleyan Chapel in 1906. St Ambrose Church, in West Cliff Road, dates from 1900 and St Alban's Church, Charminster Road, was built in 1909. The Jewish Synagogue, in Wootton Gardens, was completed in 1911.

The foundation stone for Bournemouth School for Boys in Portchester Road was laid by Lord Northbrook on 24 May 1900 and it opened a year later. Thomas George Baring, 1st Earl of Northbrook (1851–1904), was Viceroy of India in the 1870s and First Lord of the Admiralty in the 1880s. He married Elizabeth Harriet Sturt from Crichel House. Bournemouth's other top school, Bournemouth School for Girls, was founded at Ascham House in Gervis Road East.

Telecommunications opened the new century with a vigour that would be sustained for the next hundred years. In 1903, Austen Chamberlain, the Postmaster General, licensed the ironmongers and electrical engineers Bayley & Sons of Poole Hill to provide live performances from orchestras and the theatre direct into subscribers' homes. Telephone lines were to carry the service.

The technology had been developed in London in 1895 by the Electrophone Company of Gerrard Street. They offered a choice of more than a dozen West End theatres as well as the Royal Albert Hall and on Sunday no less than 15 different church services. Members of the United Services Club and other eminent institutions could listen on their own headphones to important speeches of the Prime Minister, Mr Balfour.

The young town's first ex-warriors were from the Crimean campaign of 1854–56 which was fought in the peninsula of a nation we now know as Ukraine. Coincidentally, two of its pensioners – soldier John Tiller and sailor James Hollis – died within minutes of each other on Waterloo Day, 18 June 1907. Tiller is buried in St John's churchyard, Moordown, and Hollis lies in the great municipal burial ground at the Cemetery Junction.

The archaeologist Heywood Sumner (1853–1940) moved into Robert Louis Stevenson's former home, Skerryvore, in 1897. He longed, however, for a wilder landscape surrounded by antiquities and moved in 1903 with wife Agnes and their five children to Cuckoo Hill at South Gorley, near Ringwood. Having established his credentials as an excavator he returned to the town for meetings of Bournemouth Natural Science Society and became its president.

Classic story-teller Flora Thompson (1875–1947) lived in Winton during her middle years, from 1903 to 1916. Fame came with *Lark Rise*, in 1939, which extended into a trilogy on reaching Candleford 'in the flat wheat-growing northeast corner of Oxfordshire'. She was born there, at Juniper Hill, and died in Brixham, Devon.

With the death of his brother on 26 October 1906, the Revd Father Everard Aloysius Gonzaga Arundell (1834–1907), a Catholic priest in Bournemouth, became the 13th Baron Arundell of Wardour in the peerage of England and a Count of the Holy Roman Empire. The Arundells could claim to be the most ancient of Catholic families, with deeds in the muniment room at Wardour Castle taking their pedigree back to 1260, and had distinguished themselves in the Crusades. Father Everard only headed the family for nine months. He died on 11 July 1907 and the title passed to a cousin.

The author's father, Edward George Legg (1902–69), was born in Pine Road, Winton. His father, gardener Robert George Legg (1873–1915) was a choir-master at St John's Church, Moordown. Ted's mother was Alice Jane Kearley (1872–1930) from Ridge, near Wareham. She had taught in the elementary school

in the Purbeck hamlet of West Creech. E.G. Legg became Winton's cobbler and had an encyclopaedic local knowledge.

One of his earliest memories was that the suburb had been briefly provided with what he called 'Winton's own station'. Known as Meyrick Park Halt it stood on the slope east of the railway bridge, above the Central Drive and Meyrick Park Crescent, and opened on 1 March 1906. It closed in the First World War, in October 1917, 'when they stopped running the little railcars', which were rather like the modern short trains running on branch lines. In order to confirm the spot, we scoured the cutting below the trees on the slope at the west end of St Augustin's Road, and found its steps.

The Bournemouth Society of Natural Science, which had been founded in 1883, was reformed in 1904 as Bournemouth Natural Science Society. The town's naturalists played a part in saving the last wild bulbs of the Bournemouth lily (*Simethis bicolour*). They used to meet at No. 122 Old Christchurch Road and then had rooms in Granville Chambers before moving into a purpose-built headquarters in Christchurch Road. There they found the space to display wall-mounted cases of stuffed wildlife from the pre-town heath and meadows. Many of the rarities, shot by the Earls of Malmesbury and their gamekeepers, came from Hurn Court – now Heron Court School – in parkland on the other side of the Stour from Holdenhurst. There were also considerable quantities of archaeological artefacts including those from D. Chambers of No. 41 Seabourne Road, Southbourne, who presented 'specimens of great interest from the Celtic camp which he discovered at Pokesdown'.

Traders Percy Bright and John Elmes Beale acted as benefactors and Beale was succeeded as the society's president by Dr Arthur Ransome (1834–1922) of Sunnyhurst in Dean Park Road. He was an eminent author but not the Professor Arthur Ransome (1884-1967) of *Swallows and Amazons* fame. Bournemouth's Arthur Ransome, a bacteriologist specialising in hygiene and public health, was an international expert in lung disease, consumption, phthisis and sanatorium construction.

European politics came to Bournemouth in the winter of 1907. Wilhelm II, Emperor of Germany and King of Prussia, spent three weeks at Highcliffe Castle as the guest of the Honourable Edward Stuart-Wortley (1857–1934). He arrived on

18 November 1907, at Hinton Admiral railway station, and was introduced to the pleasures of Bournemouth two days later. Having visited the pleasure gardens and pier he was driven through the crowds along the newly opened Undercliff Drive.

The Kaiser's yacht moored off Bournemouth. On 28–29 November 1907 its acclaimed orchestra came ashore and entertained townspeople in the Winter Gardens. There were many excursions into the countryside, during which the Kaiser's car became stuck in the mud of a ford in what was then Millhams Lane, just below Kinson parish church. Diplomacy was also experiencing that sinking feeling.

There is another contemporary link between Bournemouth and world affairs although it took

seven decades for it to emerge from the shadows. The traitor Sir Anthony Blunt (1907-83) was the son of Revd A.S.V. Blunt, vicar of Holy Trinity in Old Christchurch Road. Young Blunt was one of the Cambridge Apostles of the 1930s, spied for the Soviets throughout the war and, after the defection of Guy Burgess and Donald Maclean, tipped off third-man Kim Philby who fled to join them in Russia.

Professor Blunt was also a leading international art expert. As Surveyor of the Queen's Pictures he was rewarded with a knighthood in 1956. Though grilled by MI5 he was allowed to retain his freedom and status until publicly unmasked, in a House of Commons statement by Prime Minister Margaret Thatcher in 1979, after which he was stripped of his title.

Boscombe Pier, seen in its heyday in a view eastwards from below the Sandhill, was the second of the town's three piers.

Southbourne Pier derelict after the double gales of 28 December 1900 and 3 January 1901.

Edwardian traffic in the Square, eastwards to Hampshire House and the Central Hotel (left), Empress Hotel (centre), and Old Christchurch Road and Gervis Place (right).

Bandsmen playing as Bournemouth Volunteers march off to summer camp, in Boer War period uniforms and bush hats, passing a poster advertising Marsh's beer at 2s.6d. (12½p) for a dozen bottles.

Children paddling and walking the plank on east beach beside Bournemouth Pier at the turn of the twentieth century.

Pier Approach and the Victorian villas of Southcliff Road rising above Exeter Road.

The new West Overcliff Drive bridging and curving its way around the chines.

The original rustic bridge across Alum Chine, said to have been the one from which Winston Churchill fell as a youth.

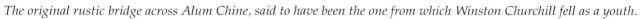

Replacement Edwardian suspension bridge at Alum Chine.

Leafy view across Alum Chine after the tree canopy engulfed the bridge.

Tuckton Bridge over the River Stour, its timbers being replaced with neat concrete arches, in 1905.

Tolstoy's books were printed in the Old Waterworks at Southbourne.

Coach party passing the newspaper offices of the Bournemouth Graphic, *in Hampshire House, between Bourne Avenue and the Square.*

C.R. Melton's Tally-Ho! *coach, beside the Pleasure Gardens, about to set off for the New Forest.*

Hands and hats raised for General William Booth of the Salvation Army as he enters the Square, in a view looking towards Exeter Road (behind tramcars) and fruiterers Leverett & Frye Ltd (top right).

The Square, northwards to Hampshire House, the spire of Punshon Memorial Church, Central Hotel and Empress Hotel.

Christchurch Road, Boscombe, between the Palmerston Arms Hotel (left) and Tom Lampard's drapery store (right).

Usher's ales on sale in Charminster House in Charminster Road in 1903.

Winton views, clockwise, from St Mark's Church in Talbot Village (top left), to Moordown lych-gate, Bryanstone Road, Talbot Woods and Wimborne Road.

A carter plods by, passing a road ganger and his wheelbarrow, beside St Stephen's Church.

Bournemouth tramcar No. 6 (on the Poole route) passing an automobile in Southbourne.

Double-headed Bournemouth Express *of the London & South Western Railway heading for the seaside.*

Up-train (right), for London Waterloo, pulling out of Bournemouth Central Station in 1905.

Railwayman releasing a cloud of homing pigeons from the goods yard behind Southcote Road.

Bournemouth Horse Show at Ensbury Park Racecourse in 1906.

Work proceeding on the construction of East Cliff Lift in the autumn of 1907.

Looking down half-built East Cliff Lift to the end of the first length of Undercliff Drive (centre right) as it nears completion in 1907.

Mayor J.A. Parsons cuts the ribbon to open the Undercliff Drive, eastwards from Bournemouth Pier to East Cliff Lift, on 6 November 1907.

Mayoress Mrs Parsons 'christening' the new Undercliff Drive, on steps below the construction site for East Cliff Lift, on 6 November 1907.

Shelters below East Cliff, towards East Cliff Hall (centre), the mansion which Sir Merton Russell-Cotes gave to the town.

East Cliff Hall becoming the Russell-Cotes Museum, after being given to the town by Merton Russell-Cotes in 1908.

Pensive young lady in the collection of Sir Merton Russell-Cotes, who was knighted in 1909.

Display cases around the dining room of Bournemouth Natural Science Society in Christchurch Road.

Otter – one of the Bournemouth exhibits, though not a Stour specimen as the label states that it is from the River Tivey, Cardiganshire.

Bittern – probably one of those shot at Hurn.

Dartford warbler – denizen of the Dorset heaths, almost eliminated by hard winters in the 1960s.

Hoopoe – among the most colourful and exotic of summer visitors.

Red squirrel – the native species of Bournemouth's pines, now restricted to Brownsea Island.

Whooper swan – winter visitor, 'shot near Heron Court, 20 January 1891'.

Concert in the Winter Gardens with the message that 'Silence is requested during the performance of each item'.

Bournemouth Pier in the summer of 1907, looking inland to the spire of St Peter's Church (centre).

Beach entertainments and the sands in a view southeastwards from below Southcliff Road in 1907, with a warship (top right) anchored offshore.

The Shelters, East Cliff Promenade and villas of Bath Road (top left), eastwards along the half-built Undercliff Drive in 1907.

Pier Approach and the Victorian villas of South Cliff Road (right) looking westwards from the Shelters beside Undercliff Drive in 1907.

Undercliff Drive (far left) and East Cliff Promenade (centre), westwards to South Cliff Road (centre) and Exeter Road (top right).

Bournemouth Square, eastwards to Hampshire House and Punshon Memorial Church (top left), the Central Hotel and Empress Hotel (centre), with tramcar No. 72 (right) heading towards Commercial Road, in the summer of 1907.

Fountain in the Lower Gardens still squirting (top) despite being surrounded by rocks of ice 'during the spell of cold weather' in the winter of 1907.

'The Man in the Iron Mask' – who walked around the world without taking it off or revealing his identity – was in Old Christchurch Road on 2 March 1908.

Newly completed East Cliff Lift, with a pair of electrically operated cable-cars (top), received its first snow on 25 April 1908.

East Cliff Lift in operation, after the building of a stronger retaining wall (centre left), in the 1920s.

Spring snow covering the main span of Bournemouth Pier on 25 April 1908.

The Square, eastwards to the Cadena Cafe, Empress Hotel and Old Christchurch Road, after the snow-storm of 25 April 1908.

The Lower Gardens in the white-out of 25 April 1908.

A truly black-and-white view of Invalids' Walk after the 1908 blizzard.

Southeastwards in the blizzard from the Central Gardens to Hampshire House and the Empress Hotel (top left).

The tramcars got through on 25 April 1908, with this one heading eastwards along Christchurch Road towards Boscombe.

Crowds in Avenue Road and a fire engine in attendance, 'very soon after the accident' at 7 pm on 1 May 1908 with tramcar No. 72 partly out of sight (centre).

Disaster postcard featuring driver William Wilton (bottom left) and the Bournemouth tram crash of 1 May 1908.

The wreckage of tramcar No. 72 in which seven passengers died, in the trees beside Avenue Road, on 1 May 1908.

'Some of the victims' and 'the curve showing where the ill-fated car left the metals' (left) on May Day in 1908.

Edwardian fashions paraded and promenaded along the decking of Bournemouth Pier.

Steamer turnstile (far left) on the west side of Bournemouth Pier, advertising trips to Swanage on the Lord Elgin *and visits by the* Balmoral *and* Lorna Doone.

Runner (centre) in Bournemouth Marathon Race, jogging along Christchurch Road, Boscombe, on 29 August 1908.

Girls' drill, with the Union Flag, at a Children's Festival in Meyrick Park.

Bournemouth Volunteer Fire Brigade attended the Children's Festival in Meyrick Park, where lads queued for their turn on the jumping sheet.

Boscombe Catholics celebrating the feast of Corpus Christi on 13 June 1909.

The 'new Technical Institute' at the Lansdowne, better known as Bournemouth Municipal College.

Edwardian last rites with clergy, flowers and horse-drawn hearse leaving for Boscombe Cemetery from St James's Church, Pokesdown.

3: WORLD WAR

The end of an era was marked by the biggest crowd that Bournemouth Square had ever seen. There was no spare standing room anywhere as a slow and melancholy 'memorial ceremony' processed into Old Christchurch Road, to St Peter's Church, after the death of King Edward VII. Prince Bertie was born on 9 November 1841 and visited the Bath Hotel as a teenager. He returned to the town to establish a love-nest with Lillie Langtry, and ascended the throne on the death of his mother, on 22 January 1901. A good decade closed with the death of Edward the Peacemaker on 6 May 1910.

Two months later, with a series of processions and fêtes in July 1910, Bournemouth celebrated its supposed centenary. The occasion marked the buying of 8 acres between the rustic bridge at the Square and Bourne Mouth – now Exeter Road – for £200, for the building of a four-roomed cottage by Captain Lewis Tregonwell (1758–1832) from Cranborne Lodge, Cranborne, Dorset. The Bournemouth cottage was kept for Tregonwell by a servant, named Symes, and became enlarged into Portman Lodge. It survived until 1930, when *The Times* reported that its levelling had revealed a smugglers' hole:

The underground chamber now discovered is about 10 feet long, 7 feet wide, and 6 feet high, and the only entrance to it is a trap door. It is a kind of arched chamber and was found about three feet below the level of the ground. When the earth and sand were cleared away from the sides of the walls they collapsed and the space it occupied has now been filled in.

Though it coincided with the Georgian discovery of the coast, Portman Lodge also dates from the peak danger period of the French Wars, which brought Tregonwell on militia duties to the seaside at Bourne Mouth. Smugglers were the normal clientele of this remote spot. At times the beach must have swarmed with men and boats, such as in 1821, when Customs seizures comprised 130 tubs of spirits in March, followed by 42 kegs of brandy and gin in October. Portman Lodge was the closest building. There were others, however, in the vicinity and two of them were much older. Decoy House stood beside the Bourne Stream and the Tapps Arms was on the corner of Old Christchurch Road and Post Office Road. Cliff Cottage, overlooking Bourne Mouth, was built in 1812.

Flying to meet the Man in the Moon was the theme of one of the winning floats in Bournemouth Centenary Carnival. Eyes lifted to closer skies as the world's leading aviators assembled their machines beside a line of hangars at Southbourne and thrilled the town. 'Flying at Bournemouth' made national headlines, such as in the *Manchester Guardian* on 15 July 1910, with the focus of attention being Claude Grahame-White 'in the course of a flight with a lady passengers'. Another popular hero was self-styled 'Colonel' Samuel Franklin Cody, an American, who made Britain's first officially recognised powered flight on 16 October 1908. He became a British citizen.

Bournemouth also made aviation history, with a tragedy, on the second day of the meeting. The last flight of biplane No. 18 is commemorated by a plaque in the school grounds in St Catherine's Road. The Honourable Charles Stewart Rolls (1877–1910), the first half of the famous Rolls-Royce partnership, stalled his French-built Wright Flyer and fell with it to his death on 12 July 1910. While attempting to land in front of the grandstand, approaching at an altitude of 70 feet, he was caught by a cross-wind and found himself too high. Attempting to correct this, he put his nose down sharply, which caused the elevator to snap. Rolls broke his neck in the crash and died instantly.

His unenviable record was to be the first victim in Britain of powered flight. Only a month before, between 18.30 and 19.18 hours on 2 June 1910, he had been the first person to fly from England to France. Then he flew back again, to Broadlees near Dover, and became the first to make a non-stop two-way crossing as he landed beside his starting-rail at 20.06 hours. This also brought the third record of being the first person to land his aeroplane without damage at a pre-arranged spot.

As well as the excitements of the centenary celebrations, 1910 marked a milestone in its own right, when James Edward Cooper Dean (1840–1921) of Littledown House granted Boscombe

Football Club a tenancy of wasteland beside King's Park. It became Dean Park.

Coronation Avenue in Moordown was named for the coronation of King George V and Queen Mary on 22 June 1911. Its principal buildings, opened that year, were the three departments of Winton and Moordown School.

Henry Hattatt Emmott of Midlothian in St Michael's Road, a well-known Bournemouth resident, was found dead on a bed in his house on 8 July 1911. Beside the fifty-six-year-old was his dog, also dead, and gas was escaping from a hole in a pipe. A bradawl lay on the floor. Letters showed that his wife had recently left him after domestic differences.

The death of Mrs Elizabeth Rebecca Johnson of the Hotel Metropole, at the Lansdowne, took place on 14 February 1912. 'I wish my funeral to be conducted liberally and regardless of expense,' she had instructed. Its cost was no problem, because as the widow of Revd John Fairbairn Johnson, she left an estate of £275,738 net, attracting tax of £55,000, and had bequeathed £135,000 to charity. Mr Johnson had been the vicar of Ab Kettleby with Holwell, near Melton Mowbray in Leicestershire.

A footnote to musical history apparently took place in Bournemouth. Sir Edward Elgar (1857–1934), at the height of his fame and already the greatest British composer since Henry Purcell, conducted his newly completed Second Symphony at a special concert in the Winter Gardens on 9 March 1912. Fellow composers Eric Coates and Sir Alexander Mackenzie credited Dan Godfrey and Bournemouth for introducing Elgar to a new hobby. A messenger boy kept bringing and taking away slips with whispers such as 'Two-thirty' and 'Three o'clock'.

On being told he was wrong to think they were discussing train times, Elgar was persuaded by the name of Steve Donoghue to hand Godfrey five shillings, moments before taking up his baton. On coming down from the platform he was told that he was £1-5s-0d richer. Elgar became a regular punter for the rest of his life.

While recovering from pneumonia, in 1912, David Herbert Lawrence (1885–1930) booked into the Royal Bath Hotel and wrote part of his novel *The Trespassers*. He was taken 'on the razzle' by a thirty-year-old 'well-built Yorkshireman with plenty of cash'. Lawrence, with a much smaller frame,

failed to keep up and resorted to pouring drink on the floor. It proved to be a pivotal moment as Lawrence the schoolmaster left Bournemouth as Lawrence the author. By 1914 he was married to Frieda von Richthofen, sister of German air-ace Baron Manfred von Richthofen, the divorced former wife of Ernest Weekley.

Having made aviation history by winning a seaplane competition in Monaco, Henry Farman's 70-horse-power Waterplane (otherwise known as the Hydroplane) landed beside Bournemouth Pier on a flight sponsored by the *Daily Mail* in the summer of 1912. On the sands, Baby Jumbo represented the competition, with the elephant and handlers collecting cash for the *Daily Mirror*'s 'Christmas pudding fund'.

Bournemouth Central Library moved from Dean Park Road in March 1913 to a matching extension of the new Technical Institute – otherwise known as Bournemouth Municipal College – at the Lansdowne. Suburban branch libraries were provided across the town by the Scottish-American steel manufacturer and philanthropist Andrew Carnegie (1835–1919).

The town's hero was bathing-machine proprietor William Tyne who jumped into the sea to save a drowning person on 1 August 1913. It was the second life he had saved within a year. In the past, around the world, Mr Tyne had saved a total of 91 bathers and swimmers who were in difficulties. The Royal Humane Certificate was awarded in recognition of his bravery.

There would soon be heroism on a wholly different scale from across the globe. The famous words of Sub-Lieutenant Rupert Brooke (1887–1915) were penned in one of the huts of C-Lines at Blandford Camp where he trained with the Anson Battalion of the Royal Naval Division:

If I should die, think only this of me:
That there's some corner of a foreign field
That is for ever England…

Before the European cataclysm, he holidayed in Bournemouth with his grandfather, Revd Richard England Brooke, at Grantchester Dene in Littledown Road. The house still stands but has become No. 48 Dean Park Road, since the inner relief road sliced through its neighbours and separated it from the rest of the street. 'Here Rupert Brooke Discovered Poetry,' its plaque reads.

That is something of an exaggeration, for Rupert was born into an academic environment, as the son of a master at Rugby. Having graduated to Cambridge, and travelled to America and New Zealand, he found Bournemouth disappointing and unexciting. It was full of 'moaning pines' and 'decrepit and grey-haired invalids' drifting 'wanly along the cliffs'. He was far more impressed with Lulworth which he praised as the most beautiful place in England.

Bournemouth provided the last holiday for the remarkable Isaac Rosenberg (1890–1918) from Stepney whose career as a private soldier also terminated with long-lasting fame as a war poet. He stayed with the Cohen family at No. 195 Wimborne Road, on the north side of Peters Hill, Winton, in 1914. Years ago a friend had some postcards that had been sent to Isaac in Bournemouth though by the time I realised their significance he had sold them for a few pence.

Christ Church, in Alumhurst Road, was completed in 1914. Work also started on St Birinus Mission Church, in Easter Road, Moordown. A concrete building, designed by Frederick A. Ling, this was described as 'plain and happy, solid and enduring'. At the dedication service on 11 April 1915, the Venerable William Andrewes Fearon, Archdeacon of Winchester, expressed pleasure that something had been done 'to rescue the Apostle of Wessex from oblivion'. Half a century later he was forgotten again, after the building had been sold by the Church Commissioners, becoming the Martin Luther Kirche in 1963. To the horror of its last vicar, Revd Reuben Henthorne, the church cleaner and caretaker went with the building and gave lifelong friendship to former enemies. The defector was my mother.

Even as the first of the world wars was brewing, Bournemouth massed for a moral cause, in the middle of June 1914. Nell, writing from 138 Wimborne Road, described it on a postcard to her cousin, sent to Mr and Mrs Symes in the Police Station at Moreton, near Dorchester:

Last Wednesday we had a large temperance demon-stration in Meyrick Park, 2300 children taking part. We marched through the town. This card represents a small portion of the crowd. Noticed PC Dreadnought on duty [underscored as a private joke]. The Band of Hope I help in took first prize for the most orderly and best marshalled society.

The campaign against drink was led by Revd Joseph David Jones of Richmond Hill Congregational Church, the great defender of the 'Bournemouth Sunday'. His was the voice of Welsh fundamental-ism against 'all vulgarities' on Sunday including day-trippers, running, opening cinemas and having bars in the new Pavilion. To many of us he had too much of his own way and created the most boring day of the week. My father, although totally non-religious, was among his successes as he 'signed the pledge' and never touched alcohol again.

Though it was of no interest to my contemporaries – whose culture was based upon the Second World War – most of my uncles experienced their war in the trenches of a generation earlier. Our family was from this other age. My mother gave birth to me as 'a mistake' in her forty-fourth year in 1947. Her father would talk of his friends going off to the Boer War and of his father's friends who failed to return from Sebastapol. It was almost Hardyesque that he recalled with particular pride a great-uncle who had served under Nelson at the Battle of the Nile. From the other side of the family we had the framed helmet badge of an Edward Legg, apparently from Tolpuddle, who fought at Waterloo.

For uncle Frank Watts who lived in The Grove at Moordown, with lungs pitted by the chlorine gas-attack at Ypres – 'Wypers' they called it – and a body still carrying a bullet and bits of shrapnel, there would still be a full working life, up ladders as a painter, and a reasonable old age. More recently, shortly before he died in 1989, another uncle recalled Passchendaele in 1917 and 'sharing our rations in a Christmas truce with Fritz'. He was retired railway ganger William Bennett who showed me how to load a bolt-action Lee-Enfield. 'The best rifle ever made,' he declared. There followed a demonstration of how to insert the bayonet and twist it for removal from the ribs.

Bournemouth's great send-off for the troops was a drumhead service in Meyrick Park on 4 October 1914. Key personnel had already been mobilised after 'the lights went out all over Europe' – to quote the Foreign Secretary, Sir Edward Grey – following the assassination by Serbians of Archduke Franz Ferdinand of Austria in Sarajevo, on 28 June 1914. A British Expeditionary Force, dismissed by the Kaiser as 'a contemptible little army', was mobilised and sailed for France and Belgium within weeks of the declaration of war on 4 August 1914. From the church of St John the Evangelist in Boscombe, Revd

E.C. Kennedy found himself at Bustard's Camp on Salisbury Plain, awoken by delivery of a telegram at 05.00 hours on 17 September 1914:

You have been selected for immediate foreign service. Report yourself early to-morrow morning at the War Office.

He was appointed Chaplain Major to the British Expeditionary Force, in Belgium, and was attached to the Seventh Division under Lieutenant-General Sir Henry Rawlinson. Major Kennedy recorded that All Fools' Day 1915 was celebrated by a pilot from the Royal Flying Corps flying across the German lines and dropping 'a new kind of bomb' which bounced across the trenches. He had delivered a football, on which was written:

The first of April, you blighters.

He also told the story of the man who was hit in the wrist by a bullet. 'Got it,' he shouted. 'I've been waiting for this since last August.' Then he produced a mouth-organ and played 'Home, Sweet Home'. Kennedy mused:

Who but an English Tommy could, or would, do that. No wonder that the French are puzzled by this strange composition of humanity with which they are fighting as allies.

Returning to England in the hospital ship *Carisbrooke Castle*, Major Kennedy found himself in the next bed to a German officer who observed, Napoleon-style, that 'the contemptible little army' never knew when it was beaten. Neither did the vicar from Boscombe. He cut short his recuperation to embark on a lecture tour, to Birkenhead and Liverpool, and again fell ill. After coming back home he died, within the week, on 25 October 1915. Though he had such a short war, he captured imagery 'both grave and gay' including the birdsong that punctuated 18-pounder artillery barrages 'as peacefully and merrily as in quiet English fields'.

Henry Page Croft, 1st Baron Croft (1881–1947), the town's Member of Parliament – who had represented what was still known as the Christchurch constituency since 1910 – went off to war with the 1st Battalion, the Hertfordshire Regiment. Mentioned in despatches and promoted Brigadier-General in February 1916 he was returned after the Great War, in 1918, for the new Bournemouth seat

and remained in place until 1940 when he was created Baron Croft of Bournemouth. He then sat in the Lords as Under Secretary of State for War. Lord Croft's autobiography, *My Life of Strife* was published posthumously in 1949.

Second-Lieutenant Gwilym Jones, only son of the minister of Richmond Hill Congregational Church, won the Military Cross. He was gassed while leading a platoon of the 2nd Battalion, the Cheshire Regiment, on the Western Front. Though he returned to action he was wounded again and transferred to the Royal Flying Corps where he became a ferry pilot, delivering aeroplanes from England to war zones for the remainder of the conflict. Gwilym Jones then worked in the Leverhulme plantations of the Gold Coast, West Africa, and was an honorary district commissioner. He died there of blood poisoning after skidding and falling from his motorcycle in 1923.

Two young Bournemouth men were posthumously awarded the Victoria Cross for valour. Corporal Cecil Noble, late of St Clement's School, died while serving with the Rifle Brigade at Neuve Chappelle in March 1915. Sergeant Frederick Riggs survived action in Gallipoli and on the Somme, where he won the Military Medal in 1916, but fell with the Yorks and Lancaster Regiment while leading his platoon against a German machine-gun post in 1918. He had attended Malmesbury Park School.

Sixty men from St Michael's parish failed to return from the Great War. St John's Church at Moordown also lost many of its young men. Servers Reginald Burt, George Ivamy, Cecil Frank Ivamy and Harold Frederick Thompson were killed in action, as was choirman and typesetter Charles Henry Austin. Then, when it was over, the influenza pandemic took its toll. Gunner Arthur Harris died when he was back for home leave in November 1918.

John Burden and William Laidlaw returned not only with their health but the Military Medal. Another local hero was Dr William Henry Putsey. When he died in 1922 he was said to have been the last surviving officer of HMS *Condor*, from the time of her 1882 adventure, in which Lord Charles Beresford bombarded Alexandria.

Stourfield House at Southbourne was converted by the British Legion into a sanatorium for crippled and convalescent soldiers. It was renamed Douglas House as a tribute to Field-Marshal Sir Douglas Haig.

The effects of the apocalyptic carnage of the Great War lasted equally long in the minds and lives of the collateral casualties. Aged parents grieved and talked all the more of lost sons, revered on their mantelpieces in unflattering and blurred sepia images, as the time arrived when they felt the need for help that spanned the generations.

Equally tragic were the host of lone spinsters – every street had its examples – who continued to hold on to brief memories and made no effort to replace the young men who did not return. A little love was stretched to last a lifetime.

The Great War established the primacy of the aeroplane for bombing, reconnaissance and transport, much as it had brought about the dominance of the tank in new-style mobile warfare on the ground. Just as the decade had opened with flights for fun, from Southbourne, it closed with the new era of commercial scheduled services. The inaugural flight from London to Bournemouth, to Ensbury Park Aerodrome on 4 May 1919, was made by an ex-military Handley Page 0400-type aircraft. Still carrying its Royal Flying Corps number (D8350 until re-designated as civilian G-EAAE) it was flown by Lieutenant-Colonel William Sholto-Douglas. He returned on 6 June 1919 to a mayoral reception. The chief pilot for Handley Page Transport, Sholto-Douglas also had a famous future, becoming Air Officer Commanding-in-Chief of Fighter Command in the Battle of Britain and retiring as Marshal of the Royal Air Force.

The town's War Memorial was built in the Central Gardens, below the Town Hall, which was the former Monte Dore Hotel. The conflict, remembered on Armistice Day on the eleventh hour of the eleventh day of the eleventh month, was still regarded as the Great War – 'the war to end all wars' – before diplomacy failed once again and it became renamed the First World War.

Memorial procession for King Edward VII, passing the Empress Hotel (centre), from the Square into Old Christchurch Road, on 20 May 1910.

Then (1863) and now (1910) shots of Christchurch Road, northeastwards up Boscombe Hill.

Four horses hauling an aviator from Earth as he greets the 'Man in the Moon' in Bournemouth Centenary Carnival in 1910.

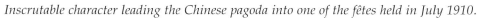

Inscrutable character leading the Chinese pagoda into one of the fêtes held in July 1910.

Chinese music-makers and their oriental float, taking part in the Bournemouth Centenary fêtes.

Horse-drawn tram taking part in Bournemouth Centenary Carnival in 1910.

J.E. Beale's 'Fancy Fair' in Old Christchurch Road decked out for the town's centenary in 1910.

The Square, garlanded for the centenary celebrations in 1910, looking westwards to Commercial Road and the London Hotel (right).

Steam-traction lorry No. 13 of White & Co. Ltd, with canvas sections for making a temporary aerodrome at Southbourne in the summer of 1910.

Cavalcade of cars, each chauffeur driven, beside Charles Stewart Rolls's hangar (left) at the aviation meeting in Southbourne in July 1910.

Self-styled 'Colonel' Samuel Franklin Cody, the American who made Britain's first officially recognised powered flight on 16 October 1908, attended Southbourne aviation meeting.

'Colonel' Cody erecting his flying-machine beside a hangar at Southbourne in July 1910.

Bleriot monoplane with an Avis machine behind, outside the hangar (far right) of George Barnes and Alan Boyle, at Southbourne Aerodrome in July 1910.

The Honourable Charles Stewart Rolls in his Wright Flyer at Southbourne in July 1910.

The fatal last flight of Charles Stewart Rolls over Bournemouth on 12 July 1910.

Stewards form a ring around the remains of the crashed aeroplane as the body of Charles Stewart Rolls is removed (right).

The twisted wreckage in which Charles Stewart Rolls made history at Bournemouth on 12 July 1910.

'Flying at Bournemouth' made headlines in the Manchester Guardian, *on 15 July 1910, with Claude Grahame-White 'in the course of a flight with a lady passenger'.*

Henry Farman's 70-horsepower Waterplane (otherwise known as the Hydroplane) taking off from below the West Cliff on a flight sponsored by the Daily Mail *in 1912.*

Aerial view of Henry Farman's Waterplane heading off into the bay in 1912.

Baby Jumbo collecting on the beach for the Daily Mirror's *'Christmas pudding fund' in the summer of 1912.*

Cyril Beale became the world's first flying Father Christmas, in Henri Salmet's two-seater Bleriot monoplane, over Bournemouth in December 1912.

The paddle-steamer Lord Elgin *approaching Bournemouth Pier from Poole Bay before the Great War.*

Paddle-steamer Brodick Castle *coming into Bournemouth with another also beginning to turn (top left).*

Brodick Castle *casting off and reversing away from Bournemouth Pier and the West Cliff.*

Bournemouth Queen *outward bound, heading eastwards, to the Solent and the Isle of Wight.*

The paddle-steamer Monarch *taking on passengers at Bournemouth Pier with the West Cliff in the background (top left).*

The paddle-steamer Emperor of India, *beside Bournemouth Pier on 1 August 1913.*

Paddle-steamer Majestic, *with an East Cliff backdrop, on 27 September 1913.*

The showmen of Bournemouth's west beach were Birchmore and Lindon's 'Gay Cadets'.

That knickerbocker moment, on Bournemouth's east beach, in a re-enactment from the era that came to an end as the world went to war.

Boys, girls and boats on the sands of Bournemouth's east beach, before the building of Undercliff Drive, overlooked by East Cliff Hall (top left).

A distinct shortage of youngsters beside the Children's Corner in the Lower Gardens, before the Great War changed
 the world.

Boscombe Blue Ribbon temperance banner (top right) and the demon drink portrayed as 'A Nation's Curse' with the
Band of Hope taking the message into the streets in 1914.

Temperance demonstrators on the march through Bournemouth in June 1914.

Bournemouth's west beach and the West Cliff, westwards from the pier to the Highcliffe Hotel (centre).

East beach, suicidally beyond use, with Bournemouth Pier surrounded by white-water as waves break over the pier-head (centre left).

Nature fights back with the newly built East Undercliff Drive awash and damaged by a storm-force gale.

Boys venture out towards the safety rail (right) between the waves as a rough sea pounds East Cliff and Bournemouth Pier (left).

Meyrick Steps, East Cliff, roped-off after cliff-falls and storm damage in 1909.

War poet Rupert Brooke was a frequent visitor to Bournemouth.

Soldier poet Isaac Rosenberg stayed with the Cohen family on Peters Hill, Winton, in 1914.

Bournemouth Pier and the town's Member of Parliament, Henry Page Croft (centre), who went off to war and was promoted Brigadier-General in February 1916.

Revd E.J. Kennedy, vicar of St John's, Boscombe, 'off to the Front' from Bournemouth Central Station.

Bournemouth troops muster for war at a drumhead service in Meyrick Park on 4 October 1914.

Wartime winter, with a scene of desolation worthy of the Western Front, in a view towards the black poplar tree in the Upper Gardens (top left) on 26 February 1916.

Driver Frost and conductor Ted Legg of Bournemouth Corporation Tramways, with two points operators, in Bournemouth Square late in 1916.

Inaugural flight from Ensbury Park Aerodrome with ex-military Handley Page 0400-D8350 (which became G-EAAE) taking off on 4 May 1919.

Mayoral reception for Lieutenant-Colonel William Sholto-Douglas, chief pilot for Handley Page Transport, who landed with Bournemouth's first scheduled commercial flight on 6 June 1919.

Armistice Day wreaths on the new War Memorial beside the Bourne Stream.

The War Memorial, also known as the Cenotaph, in the Central Gardens below the Town Hall (top right).

4: TOWERING TWENTIES

I have a postcard marked with an ink 'X' on the east side of the Zig-zag path down from the Clifton Road junction with Southbourne Overcliff Drive. The contemporary writer explained, 'This is where the murder took place on the cliffs.'

The body of Miss Irene Wilkins, a cook, was discovered just before Christmas in December 1921. She had been dead for some time. She had been inveigled down to Bournemouth, from London, by a decoy telegram sent from Boscombe Post Office. The attack had in fact taken place indoors, with blows to the head from a short poker. Her head had then been wrapped in a tablecloth to staunch the blood. The victim remained alive for some time as she swallowed a considerable amount of blood. The killer hauled her into a car and drove to the cliffs. The body was then dragged by the ankles through a barbed wire fence into the gorse bushes of a scrubby clifftop field.

The forged telegrams provided a crucial clue. More than 22,000 handwriting samples were analysed before a close comparison was found. It was criminal evidence in its own right, being a stolen cheque, and had attracted attention through the misspelling of Arthur ('Arther'). The trail led to chauffeur Thomas Henry Allaway from Windsor Road, Boscombe – who had fled to Reading. He stood trial at Winchester, in the summer of 1922, and was sentenced to death. The *Weekly Dispatch* catalogued the evidence and concluded on 9 July 1922:

> *The Bournemouth murder will go down in history as one of the finest detective stories in our criminal annals.*

As with so many other high-profile cases that generated masses of evidence, the police had already had Allaway drawn to their notice. His motor car, LK 7405, was brought to police attention as a suspect vehicle on 6 January by a Mr Humphries, but the chauffeur had 'a plausible tale' and the report was 'filed away with other papers'.

Bournemouth's population reached 90,000 in 1921. Dr Thomas Bodley Scott (1851–1924) had moved to the town from Brighton and became the primary 'medicine man' – his own term – to Bournemouth's fashionable Victorians. He married Adeline Savory and established his surgery at Aldington, Poole Road. To 'my friend Thomas Bodley Scott' Robert Louis Stevenson dedicated his *Underwoods* collection of lyric poems in 1887, for 'when next my ill-fortune brings him hurrying to me' he 'will care to remember that he takes this trouble for one who is not fool enough to be ungrateful'.

Bodley Scott wrote a book entitled *Why do we Die?* and became Mayor of Bournemouth on his retirement from medicine in November 1923. The answer in his own case to the title of his book was a bout of gastric influenza in February 1924. Having ignored what should have been his advice to himself he continued attending public events and became the town's first Mayor to die in harness.

Among the arrivals in Bournemouth was General Sir Reginald Clare Hart (1848–1931) from Netherbury in Dorset who won the Victoria Cross in the Afghan War of 1870. He became Colonel Commandant of the Royal Engineers in 1922 and retired to Beaufort House at No. 39 West Cliff Road. As a grand old man of Empire he frequently returned to the colonies to indulge his passion for big game shooting.

Boscombe Football Club and its league results were consistently poor until 1924 when the club signed up Ronnie Eyre from Sheffield Wednesday. Less than five minutes into his first game he had scored the first of what would be 200 league goals in eight and a half seasons. Things also looked up for the supporters, who were provided with a steel-framed grandstand from the site of the British Empire Exhibition at Wembley. This became Dean Park Stadium in 1927. It had seating for 3500 which was just about adequate for the average attendance of some 5000 spectators.

By 1924 the innovative telephone concert service of 1903 was being eclipsed by the latest electrical wonder – the wireless – and its 62 subscribers began defecting to the new medium. In 1927 the Royal Theatre abandoned land-line transmissions and in 1929, when the old Winter Gardens closed, the town council refused to wire the replacement Pavilion for sound, to allow the orchestra to be relayed from there. The collapse of the service left just two subscribers, Mrs Cooper and Mrs Hatchcock, receiving telephone transmissions when the plug was eventually pulled in 1938. The last such system in the country, it offered on its final Sunday four different church services, to which the ladies could listen.

Sir Dan Godfrey's son, Dan Godfrey junior, moved into the new medium and became station controller and musical director of Manchester Broadcasting Station which went into the ether as '2ZY' on 370 metres wavelength. Godfrey often stood in as the announcer.

Back in Bournemouth, call-sign '6BM' was another of the eight original stations of the British Broadcasting Corporation, to be found at 385 metres on the medium wave-band. Bertram Fryer, W.R. Keene and Ian Oliphant were among the first announcers. Talks included J.C.B. Carter on H.G. Wells and his works (in two parts), Miss M.R. Dacombe on smuggling days in Dorset, and W.J. Harding on his rambles in the cause of entomology. 'Eighty years ago' – with ninety minutes of reminiscing – sounds compelling and one wishes it could have been recorded. As with the Manchester station, however, music had primacy as national managing director John Reith ordained. The *Radio Times* of 14 December 1923 reports that Winifred Ascott was among its stars:

Miss Winifred Ascott, whose singing from Bournemouth has called forth many congratulations from listeners, has a delightful soprano voice, and her powerful notes are in direct contrast to her small personal stature, which gave rise to the following amusing story. Miss Ascott had been engaged to sing at a particularly large and important concert in a town where she was not known, and upon making her entrance she faintly heard the following comment: 'I say, paying for this, are we? We shan't get much for our money.'

Miss Ascott then proceeded to show them what big voices sometimes come from small persons. The commentator evidently had a pleasant surprise after the first verse and was foremost in the applause.

Special December programmes from Bournemouth – with partial 'simultaneous broadcast' to London ('2LO' on 363 metres) – included Flight-Lieutenant J.M. Amers conducting the Band of His Majesty's Royal Air Force. The opening voice that Sunday evening was contralto Lulu Bradshaw with the hymn 'Nearer My God to Thee' which to this day brings an image of the sinking of RMS *Titanic*. On weekdays, Bournemouth had its Women's Hour, Kiddies' Hour and alternate Boys' Brigade News and Boy Scouts' and Girl Guides' News, which at fifteen minutes each were equal in length to the national news from London.

The other capital-produced programme, of similar length, was by BBC book critic John Strachey. My earliest copy of the *Radio Times*, courtesy of an old lady in Bournemouth, has a contemporary ring in fountain-pen ink around 'Close Down' for '6BM' at 10.25 pm on Wednesday 19 December 1923. Captain W.A. Featherstone had conducted solo pianoforte Gladys Seymour, baritone Robert Sturtivant, contralto Constance Willis, tenor Harold Stroud, and soprano Edith Thomas. The final pieces, which opened with the foxtrot 'Louisville Loo' had closed with a one-step, 'Ain't got a minute'.

The journal also contains a piece of trivia that I have never seen elsewhere. It confirms that the first-ever outside broadcast, by use of a portable wireless transmitter to a studio, took place from the top of Nelson's Column on the evening of Saturday 24 November 1923. The engineer was Captain Peter Pendleton Eckersley who relayed to national radio – then based at Savoy Hill beside the Victoria Embankment – the sound of 'sparrows twittering'. Whatever the BBC achieved there, and in other directions, it is clear that in the early days of the wireless the French were much more adventurous. Their broadcasts, transmitted from the Eiffel Tower, included Parliamentary reports, racing news and stock market prices.

Back on the ground, in Bournemouth, the Catholic Church of the Annunciation in Charminster Road was designed, in Byzantine style, by Sir Giles Gilbert Scott – of K6 phone box fame – in the 1920s. It was built by Mrs Lionel Coxon in memory of her father, Lieutenant-Colonel Meyrick, of the Grenadier Guards.

One of Bournemouth's most familiar urban landmarks, the Clock Tower in the Square was presented to the town by Captain Harry B. Norton JP in 1925, in return for which a new road at Talbot Park was named in his honour. He was a dependable benefactor for town causes and donated the £400 balance necessary for St Peter's Church to pay for its new bells in 1937.

Poet and builders' merchant Kenneth Hopkins (born 1914), the son of a Bournemouth cobbler on military service in India, had his first published poem in *St Peter's Church Magazine* at the age of ten in 1925. As a choirboy he lived on the north side of Southcote Road, close to the Central Station:

Our part of Southcote Road contained bigger houses than the station end, and none of those commercial yards backing on to the railway behind our houses. In fact we backed on to the tram depot, and the railway lay behind that. So we felt (anyway, I did) that ours was a very select area.

He was born at No. 133 Southcote Road, but lived mainly at No. 41 as a baby during the First World War, then stayed nights at Aunt Ada's in No. 49 before father returned from the war and bought No. 125 which remained the family home into the second half of the twentieth century. The latter house was distinguished by its eucalyptus tree. Kenneth Hopkins left for London in 1938 and was remembered in the town for his rallying cry for the 13th Bournemouth Boy Scouts:

The 13th is the oldest troop that ever the town has known. T'was started soon after the seeds, by Baden-Powell, were sown.

Falaise, at No. 13 West Overcliff Drive, with its Adam-style fireplaces and a Channel view, became the home of pioneer aviator Sir Alan Cobham (1894–1973). He was widely known for Alan Cobham's Flying Circus and its breathtaking stunts though Sir Alan's instant knighthood was the reward for flying to Australia and back in 1926. He was the first to fly over the Himalayas and all round the coast of Africa. His legacy was in-flight refuelling which revolutionised long-distance travel as well as the waging of war.

Ensbury Park was visited in 1926 by Bert Hinkler in his Avro Avian. The following year they made a record-breaking trip to Australia where the aircraft is preserved.

Stunt flying continued at Bournemouth for another short season, until the unfortunately named Killjoy Stakes did just that with an aerial collision in full view of the stands of Ensbury Park Racecourse. In that Major L.P. Openshaw, the test pilot for Westland Aircraft Company in Yeovil, was killed on 6 June 1927. His Westland Widgeon and a Blackburn Bluebird were only feet above the ground.

One of the last of the many Bronze Age burial mounds that had studded Bournemouth's heath and plantations was excavated in July 1927. The archaeologists dismantling Thistle Barrow at King's Park were Dr and Mrs R.C.C. Clay and Colonel John Richard Dodd (1858–1930). Years later I met Dr Clay when my brother, Barrie Legg, took us to see his aquarium at Fovant, Wiltshire, but discussion was restricted to tropical fish.

For the archaeology, some of which was saved by the efforts of Sir Edwin Ray Lankester whilst president of Bournemouth Natural Science Society, it fell to Herbert Druitt (1876–1943) of the Red House, Quay Road, Christchurch, to accumulate what he could. The amount was immense – a total of 2450 boxes – samples from which were shown to me by J. Bernard Calkin, joint headmaster of Wychwood School, Braidley Road, from 1926 to 1939. The collection came into the public domain in 1951 when Druitt's sister Charlotte turned her late brother's home into the Red House Museum. Calkin said there were 140 burial mounds in the Bournemouth area:

… most of them much like Thistle Barrow with the exception of an earlier one north of Castle Lane, known as the Holdenhurst Long Barrow, which was flattened in 1936 and covered with houses.

He handed me beaker-shaped urns, hand-axes and worked flints to make his point about the wealth of prehistoric material. There were labels to the effect that some had been bought from 'Marshall the Pretender' to distinguish him from Revd Walter Marshall (1859–1921) who was vicar of Christchurch. The other Marshall, in Druitt's words, 'appeared a bit cracked' and believed that he was the Earl of Shaftesbury.

Bernard Calkin told me there was a Palaeolithic flint axe from a garden in Easter Road, found when my home was built in the 1920s, displayed in the cases of Russell-Cotes Museum. This collection was transferred to the Red House Museum in the 1960s. Calkin said 'the quantity was unique' because so much land in and around Bournemouth had been dug with hand-tools, by workers looking for antiquities which they kept until Druitt next toured around. He invariably bought them 'for the price of a drink'. Bournemouth was not only 'remarkably rich' in the range of its archaeology but finds on this scale could never be made again 'because everything now goes through machines and gets dumped elsewhere or used as hard-core'.

My parents, Gladys and Ted Legg, frequently hired a tent for either the afternoon (9d.) or whole day (1s. 3d.) below the Zig-zag path down East Cliff. Picnics were the order of the day. They brought a teapot – and their own tea – and paid threepence to have it filled with hot water. I was then told of the sensation that was Lobby Ludd.

Using this pseudonym, a reporter from the *Westminster Gazette* read the paper in a deck-chair, as he tried to pass incognito amid summertime crowds. Placards across the premier South Coast holiday resort read: 'Missing man in Bournemouth'. To win the national newspaper's promotional cash, members of the public had to challenge him with these precise words:

You are Mr Lobby Ludd and I claim the Westminster Gazette prize.

Invariably, he was not Mr Ludd; it must have ensured that the entire male population gave up reading the paper in a public place. The idea came from detective-writer Agatha Christie's mystery disappearance in 1928 with the name Lobby Ludd being a combination of the paper's telegraphic address (Lobby, for its Parliamentary associations) and the location of its London offices (Ludd, for Ludgate Circus).

Inland, at Riverside below Redhill, Hugh Marshall's Tea and Strawberry Gardens had the choice spot for picnics, overlooking the River Stour from the slopes west of the Horse and Jockey. They also ran the rope ferry, comprising a punt and a long oar, which was heaved across the river at Riddlesford with the aid of an overhead cable. Twenty people squeezed in at a time was a record load 'but a dozen at a time was safer and sensible'. It was still carrying a total of 14,000 passengers a year across to Home Meadow in Hampshire and the path in the other direction to West Parley in Dorset. Most of the 'new visitors' did not stray beyond the meadows. Further along, local boys still swam as they had for generations, swinging on ropes and leaping from high trees.

There was still a wide ford at Riddlesford, before changes in the depth and course of the river, and the riverside footpath from West Parley was still a cart-road. Used by the milkman each day, it became increasingly dangerous with the varying flows, 'but the milk always got through'. That was until horse and driver ran out of luck, losing their grip on the swirling gravel, and were swept away to their deaths.

Sargent's Bakery, in the Old Cottage, had been the first in Bournemouth and older people recalled that Redhill and Muscliffe Farm used to be 'the bread basket for the town'. The tradition of produce from the land continued with a new generation of horticulturalists. Nurseryman Arthur Dunning built double lines of heated glasshouses behind his new home at Easter Road, Moordown, and found flat and fertile ground for his market garden just above the flood plain at Throop.

Hugh Marshall (1867–1950) was the great Redhill character. As an elephant-hunter in Nyasaland and Northern Rhodesia he had surveyed a length of the proposed Cape to Cairo telegraph line for Cecil Rhodes. Returning home to Bournemouth in the 1890s he was carrying and bottle-feeding a lion cub. It grew up in the stable until being taken on a one-way visit to Bristol Zoo.

As his next companions, 'Boss' Marshall had two boys, Baruta and Kasmea who were with the native carriers at Abercorn. Marshall said they were orphans, 'taken by Arab slave-traders in Benin', whom he had personally liberated. They were certainly grateful and faithful, and with the next danger being the outbreak of the Boer War in 1899, Marshall found himself summoned to dinner in Cape Town with Rhodes. The boys refused to leave their Boss.

Marshall took them with him, had them togged-up by a tailor 'in blue suits and red fezzes' and spent a total of £250 in packing them off in the next boat to Southampton. They were given the address of brother Hugh Marshall who in turned passed them on to his parents at Redhill. Charles Marshall (1843–1908) and his wife, née Love Lawford (1843–1921) rose to the task. They found a couple of hard-tyre bicycles and sent the boys off on them each day to the 1828-built British School at Throop, which was then run by Congregational minister Revd Samuel Eldridge. By the time they left they could read and write and Mrs Marshall treasured their immaculately written thank-you letter.

Riddlesford ferry was regarded as a scenic curiosity by the 1920s. Bournemouth solicitor Edwin Dodshon captured the historic process in a series of magic-lantern slides for Bournemouth Natural Science Society. These found their way into my father's show which survived in Christmas use long enough for the equipment to be adapted for the new age of the colour transparency.

The Twenties brought high-rise living to the Bournemouth skyline but could have done so much more. As money multiplied on the world stock exchanges, London department-store magnate Gordon Selfridge, who had Highcliffe Castle at Christchurch as his holiday home, decided to build something much bigger. He bought Hengistbury Head and employed architect Philip Tilden to draw up plans for a Highcliffe-sized Little Castle, in which he would live, while a palace-sized Large Castle was built over the following two or three decades. The Gothic pile was to be surrounded by four miles of walls and bastions.

It was not only going to be Britain's biggest house of the twentieth century but had to be nothing less than 'the largest house in the world'. At its centre was a dome just 10 feet less in diameter than that of St Paul's Cathedral. Beside it the drawings show an even higher battlemented tower. 'They will have learnt to laugh with joy, not derision, when it is accomplished,' Tilden mused.

Fellow businessmen Sir Thomas Lipton and Sir Ernest Cassell stood with the American Solicitor-General, James Montgomery Beck, on Hengistbury Head. Hundreds of drawings were spread across the floor of Highcliffe Castle. They showed a thousand rooms for guests, in suites of four for each visitor, comprising a bedroom, dressing-room, bathroom and sitting-room. Gordon Selfridge promised to bring Beck and his friends across the Atlantic in a specially commissioned ocean liner that would dock in Southampton.

In the event, Bournemouth's notable building of the decade was the new Pavilion, which was opened by the Duke of Gloucester on 19 March 1929. The Selfridge dream had collapsed with the Wall Street Crash in October 1929.

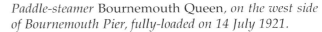

Rescue boat off West Cliff fund-raising for 'Lifeboat Saturday' on 21 August 1920.

Paddle-steamer Bournemouth Queen, *on the west side of Bournemouth Pier, fully-loaded on 14 July 1921.*

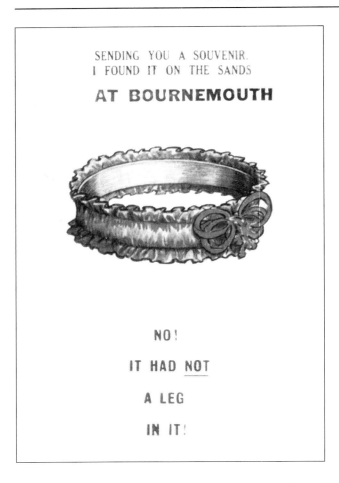

SENDING YOU A SOUVENIR.
I FOUND IT ON THE SANDS

AT BOURNEMOUTH

NO!

IT HAD NOT

A LEG

IN IT!

The postwar saucy seaside postcard began with Bamforth's 'Comic Series'.

Private bathing tents – the exclusive corner of west beach – in a view southeastwards to Bournemouth Pier in the 1920s.

East beach at its widest, in an extreme low tide, looking northwestwards to the Highcliffe Hotel in the 1920s.

The pond at the heart of Queen's Park (centre left) in a setting that catered for amphibians as well as golfers.

Queen's Park and its golf course, downhill from Holdenhurst Road (now Littledown Drive) to the newt pond (centre left) in the 1920s.

Bournemouth Municipal Orchestra and their Winter Gardens concert hall, in the 1920s, after conductor Sir Dan Godfrey received his knighthood.

Dan Godfrey junior left Bournemouth for Manchester to control Broadcasting Station '2ZY'.

Beales & Sons delivery men and their van in 1924.

Global flyer and in-flight refuelling pioneer Sir Alan Cobham.

Falaise, facing seawards at No. 13 West Overcliff Drive, became the home of Sir Alan Cobham.

Twenties-style picnic, beneath a wing, for Sir Alan and Lady Gladys Cobham.

Bournemouth Square, eastwards to the Empress Hotel (left) and Gervis Place (centre), with the tram (right) heading for County Gates, Westbourne, in the 1920s.

East beach, crowded once more, seen from Bournemouth Pier in the 1920s.

West beach and Bournemouth Pier with a tented ice-cream kiosk (centre) and wheeled landing-stages behind.

Boscombe Chine Gardens in the snow in 1925.

Bert Hinkler taking off from Ensbury Park Aerodrome in 1926, a year before making a record-breaking flight to Australia where his Avro Avian is preserved.

Westland test pilot Major L.P. Openshaw passing the Racecourse stands at Ensbury Park Aerodrome moments before being killed in a collision on 6 June 1927.

Thistle Barrow, King's Park, with archaeologists Dr R.C.C. Clay, Colonel J.R. Dodd and Mrs Clay on 19 July 1927.

Colonel J.R. Dodd and the half-excavated Thistle Barrow at Boscombe – a Bronze Age burial mound – in July 1927.

Tents on the beach at the bottom of the Zig-zag, East Cliff, with Ted and Gladys Legg (centre background) enjoying a picnic in 1928.

Bournemouth Pier and the Pier Approach in the mid-1920s, from Bournemouth Aviation Company's passenger-carrying Avro biplane.

Lady Morris laying the foundation stone for the extended home of Bournemouth Natural Science Society, in Christchurch Road, on 8 July 1929.

The rope ferry at Riddlesford, across the River Stour, between Redhill and West Parley, was still in use in the 1920s.

The Stour providing a riverside idyll in the 1920s.

The new Pavilion, from the south, looking across the Lower Gardens in June 1928.

Children's Corner, down the Bourne Stream to the Bandstand and Pavilion in 1928.

The Pavilion (left) and Bath Road up to the Royal Bath Hotel (centre) northeastwards across Pier Approach from East Cliff Promenade (foreground) in 1929.

5: TROUBLED THIRTIES

Bournemouth's penultimate land grab took place in 1930 with the acquisition of the Dorset parish of Kinson including the northwestern suburbs of Ensbury Park, Northbourne, Wallisdown, East Howe, West Howe and Bearwood. Then, in the southeastern extremity of what could now be called '7 miles of golden sands', cartographical neatness was achieved by the purchase of Hengistbury Head. Christchurch relinquished parochial control and a new boundary line was drawn across Christchurch Harbour.

The Church of England also continued to redraw its maps, notably to create a parish for St Francis of Assisi Church which was erected on top of the hill overlooking Broadway Lane and Throop, in 1930. It has a 125-feet tower, rising from a flight of steps above Charminster Road, topping off a striking Italian-style building which was designed by J. Harold Gibbons.

A couple of decades later it dominated my Sundays in the time of Revd Julian Rudd who had me confirmed as one of his flock. As the regular workhorse who replaced kneelers, prayer books and hymn books after services, I was once taken to task by an elderly lady for trotting along each row of seats as I performed the task. 'How irreverent,' she snapped. 'Do not run in church!'

I remonstrated with what, even after another half century of practice, is still among my best retorts: 'Why shouldn't the Lord's work be done efficiently?'

Flying ace Amy Johnson (1903–41) landed in her Gypsy Moth to a hero's welcome at Talbot Farm on 27 August 1930. She arrived to open a fête in Meyrick Park and was met by Sir William Morris in his best six-cylinder automobile which he gave to her as a present. Four months earlier she became the first woman to fly solo from Britain to Australia. En route she had also broken the record for a flight to India, by landing in Karachi, six days out from London.

Rail transport reacted to the coming age of competition by introducing luxury services. From 1931 until the end of the steam era in 1967, the Pullman coaches of the *Bournemouth Belle* provided a combination of catering and comfort that were the equal of a top-class hotel. The *Golden Arrow* and *Brighton Belle* offered equivalent delights – against the clock in the case of Brighton where travelling time tended to be too short – but Bournemouth was the famous route. Not only was this 'the most elegant of Pullman trains' but it was 'the most handsome train in Britain'. Film stars, businessmen and the plain rich came and went in style between Waterloo and Bournemouth Central Station.

Growing up in Bournemouth at this time was the comedian Tony Hancock (1924–68) who had moved from Birmingham at the age of three. His nanny was my Aunt Maud, a courtesy title for Mrs Skivington, of Easter Road. She looked after him until he was sent to Durlston Court School in Swanage where he became introverted and withdrawn at the onset of puberty. After acting during the war with the RAF Gang Show he returned to all our lives, through radio, television and films.

A chain-smoking perfectionist, called 'the anxiety man' by the newspapers, he always found it difficult to incorporate women into his act. As with many great comedians, he took professional humour desperately seriously, and was prone to bouts of depression. He killed himself while on tour in Sydney in 1968.

Tragic Alma Victoria Rattenbury (1897–1935) lost her husband to a knock on the head with a mallet from her lover, George Percy Stoner (born 1916), and faced a joint murder trial at the Old Bailey. The killing took place at Villa Madeira, No. 5 Manor Road, in March 1935. Stoner had responded to an advertisement the previous September for a … 'Daily willing lad, 14–18, for housework. Scout-trained preferred.'

He became the chauffeur to Francis Mawson 'Ratz' Rattenbury, and took up residence, embarking upon a passionate affair with his wife. Mrs Rattenbury was acquitted but Stoner was sentenced to death on 31 May 1935 by Justice Christmas Humphreys. Four days later, she committed suicide, stabbing her breasts six times, on the river bank of a tributary of the River Avon west of Stony Lane, Christchurch.

The spot, below a railway bridge, was where she had made love to Stoner. A cowman, William Charles Mitchell, saw her final moments but was unable to pull her from the water. 'If only I thought it would help Stoner I would stay on,' she had written, 'but it has been pointed out to me all too vividly that I cannot help him.'

Ironically, though Stoner's appeal was dismissed on 24 June 1935, the Home Secretary responded the following day to a 100,000-name petition for leniency. Stoner was reprieved. He was released from prison in 1942, and returned after the war to Redhill Drive, where he spent an uneventful rest of his life with his wife Christine.

In November 1935, Sir Dan Godfrey returned to the rostrum at the Winter Gardens, in the 1876-built glasshouse, to conduct Bournemouth Municipal Orchestra. It was a farewell to the old building, which was to be demolished that winter, and eventually replaced by a functional brick hall.

Bearded antiquarian bookseller Alan Gradon Thomas (1911–92) ran the shop trading as Horace G. Cummin, in Old Christchurch Road, between the times of Ernest Cooper and John Ruston. Thomas lived at Wimborne with his first wife, Ella, but moved to Chelsea in 1965 to establish himself as the doyen of the British antiquarian book trade.

In the 1930s, on Bournemouth beach, he had spent happy times with Thomas and Lawrence Durrell. The latter dedicated his second novel *Panic Spring* to Thomas in 1937, and was relieved that in return the self-taught bookseller read the proofs for him. The book was published under the pseudonym Charles Norden owing to poor sales of his first novel.

Medicine and hygiene are often only faltering steps ahead of the bugs that continually probe our defences. They tend to strike when our guard is down and can return us within hours to conditions that are Victorian England at its grimmest. Usually, these days, it is on a foreign holiday when one is most vulnerable. But before the age of overseas travel, when Bournemouth was about as far south as the masses could venture, it was there that the worst nightmare struck.

It was at the peak of the season, in high summer in 1936, when the resort started to experience the worst publicity of its existence. The August bank holiday then fell earlier than now, at the second weekend in

the month, and it was at this most unfortunate of times that an outbreak of pyrexia, an unidentified fever, was reported from the Durley Dean Hotel and households in the prestigious West Cliff area. It spoiled many holidays and was followed, in the ten days to 22 August, by a spate of cases of suspected enteric fever.

Some 100 people were admitted to hospitals in Bournemouth and Poole. Medical opinion was revised and the fever was given the more ominous title of paratyphoid. Worse, however, was to come. On 24 August, laboratory tests confirmed that the fever raging in Bournemouth was the real thing – typhoid!

Hundreds, if not thousands, of people were now thought to be in danger. Indeed, the number of cases rose to over 700, involving holidaymakers and residents alike. Suspicion fell upon the milk they were drinking, because all appeared to have been supplied from Froude's Dairy in The Triangle. Nothing implicated their methods or cleanliness but the trail was narrowed to the unpasteurised supply, and in particular one being collected from a farm near Wimborne.

Thousands were in fact in mortal peril, because Froude's supplied a quarter of the town; more than 10,000 households.

The clinching piece of evidence then came from Wimborne, where a farmer's wife became dangerously ill, and died from typhoid on 8 September. A judicial inquiry into the Bournemouth typhoid epidemic, in which a total of 51 would die, heard in February 1937 that the late Dr Vernon Shaw, who had died in December 1936 from unrelated causes, had traced the bacillus to a stream on the farm. A drain emptied into it, allowing sewage to seep into the stream, from which cows carried the disease to the farmer's wife and then, via contaminated milk, to Froude's Dairy and a quarter of Bournemouth.

The sewer pipe led to Merley House. This impressive pile had been the seat of sugar and rum magnate Ralph Willett (1719–95), owner of a slave plantation on the Caribbean island of St Christopher's – now St Kitts – on the slopes of its aptly named Mount Misery.

Willett, of the family commemorated by the rebuilt Willett Arms roadhouse, which used to be thatched, built Merley House in the 1850s. He had as little as possible to do with his slaves and instead ploughed his wealth into the London second-hand book market, collecting on a massive scale and enlarging the classical house with two wings in 1772, principally to house his burgeoning library.

This was the unlikely setting where Dr Shaw tracked his errant bacterium to ground and came up with a suspect who had also travelled extensively in the tropics.

Sixteen members of the household were examined and the carrier identified. Merley House was then owned by Captain Angus Valdimar Hambro JP (1883–1957) who was educated at Eton and had played golf for England: politics too, as MP for South Dorset from 1910 to 1922, serving as Parliamentary Private Secretary to the Air Minister in the closing stages of the First World War.

Some of the surviving victims also became carriers and were not released from isolation hospital for more than a year. The ordeal would plague their lives and typhoid bacilli continued to be found in samples from Poole's sewers into the 1960s. It was also found alive, at *post mortem* investigations, in the lower intestines and gall-bladders of elderly carriers who had just died from other causes.

Few in Bournemouth needed convincing of the wisdom in changing to bland but safe pasteurised milk. The story is also a cautionary tale for our times in showing that even in clean-living country house Dorset and streets of clifftop hotels the perils of the past can still return to haunt us.

Fresh, non-heated 'straight from the cow' raw milk and cream is topical again, as the Government makes yet another attempt at banning what we now know as green-topped milk.

During the 1930s the times were changing for several institutions. St Peter's Vicarage, where my mother was a maid to the Green-Wilkinson family, was sold for £31,000 in 1931 and was replaced on the site by the apartments of Bath Hill Court. The vicar persuaded Sir George Meyrick, patron of the parish and titular owner of the land, to set aside his interest in the ground but the deal won the Church authorities few friends. Church historian and solicitor Ian McQueen records that 'even the Bishop had second thoughts', and my mother lamented the loss 'of that lovely house' for the rest of her life.

'We have become a parish of boarding houses and hotels,' said the Revd Hubert Marsh as he prepared to retire from St Peter's Church to a rural living. Despite the sale, financial problems continued and St Peter's School, founded in 1850, closed in 1935. The new vicar, Revd Hedley Burrows, found that this time the parish would receive nothing for the land, as the Meyrick Estate trustees had the right to reversion of title if and when it ceased to be used for educational purposes. The extensive town centre site became Maples store and a block of flats in 1938.

Lansdowne School, dating from 1875, also closed in 1935 and its site in Madeira Road was earmarked for the new Central Police Station. The Bournemouth School moved from Portchester Road to new red-brick buildings facing East Way, Charminster, in 1939.

The distant drums of war, which was finally triggered by events 'in a far-away country about which we know nothing', were already seen as an inevitability to those who followed the rise of German militarism. 'No Arms for Nazis' was painted on Lady Wimborne's bridge, crossing Ringwood Road at Alderney, and remained visible on the concrete underside until its demolition in about 1970. Lieutenant-Colonel Arthur Malim was scathing in February 1939 about the attractions of the blue-and-scarlet uniform of the Auxiliary Fire Brigade to young men who should have been joining him in the Territorial Army:

We can supply the uniform, not blue with scarlet facings, but His Majesty's khaki. That is where the young men of Bournemouth ought to be – not running around with hosepipes. It will be a bad day for Bournemouth and other towns if they cannot get men to take an active part in a battalion of His Majesty's Army, as part of the field force that will defend the lives and liberties of the people when the time comes. Fit young men of the right age ought to be in the Territorial Army – not in those organisations which are all very well for old men who are not fit.

In the event, it was the reorganised structure of the town's fire service in 11 zones, each with its emergency fire station, that saw action first in the Second World War before a British shot was fired. The mobilisation of the British Army started on Saturday 2 September, ahead of Prime Minister Neville Chamberlain's broadcast to the nation from the Cabinet room in No. 10 Downing Street. It was raining again. 'It's raining everywhere,' the King had said, laconically, as he reviewed the Fleet at Weymouth three weeks earlier.

The 750 firemen and 26 firewomen of Bournemouth's Auxiliary Fire Service were called up for duty and were kept on the go answering 15 flood calls between 21.45 hours that Saturday and 01.35 hours on that day that war would be declared. Bobby's department store in the Square had to be pumped out, with the loss of two tons of sugar, as did a newly constructed air-raid shelter. Electrical transformers exploded and the Pier Approach Baths found itself with an embarrassment of water in its basement. Its swimming pool, however, holding 150,000 gallons, was now designated as an emergency reservoir for fire-fighting purposes.

That morning, as sunshine followed the rain and the nation went to church, advance notice of the declaration of war hummed through military communication lines at ten o'clock. It was followed by the fateful broadcast to the nation at 11.15:

This morning the British Ambassador in Berlin handed the German Government a final note stating that unless we heard from them by eleven o'clock that they were prepared at once to withdraw their troops from Poland a state of war would exist between us. I have to tell you now that no such undertaking has been received and that consequently this country is at war with Germany.

Newly built Bournemouth Corporation Baths (centre), in a view eastwards from Pier Approach, up Bath Road to the Royal Bath Hotel.

East beach and the Royal Bath Hotel (top centre) eastwards along East Cliff in the 1930s.

The Shelters and Beach Cafe, with Edgar Lewis's boarding house and those of Lynwood and Kildare beside Bath Road (centre), overlooked by Palace Court Hotel (top left).

Undercliff Drive (bottom left), seen from East Cliff, with bathing huts beside it and a children's climbing frame bridging a pool of water below the tideline.

The new coastal skyline of the 1930s, northeastwards from Bournemouth Pier to the Pavilion (centre), Bournemouth Corporation Baths and Palace Court Hotel (top right).

Bournemouth Pier (foreground), northwards to the Lower Gardens and Westover Road (centre) after completion of the Pavilion and Pier Approach Baths (lower right) in 1930.

From 2000 feet above East Cliff, this view is northeastwards from the Carlton Hotel (lower right) and Meyrick Road to the roads radiating from the Lansdowne (centre) and the town's Central Station (centre top).

Middle Chine and its beach, with the West Overcliff Drive skirting it above, and a newly constructed promenade reaching it from below.

Middle Chine became the town's most scenic car park in the 1930s.

Bournemouth Fire Brigade attending to an overheating motor car in 1932.

LJ 580, known as 'The Flyer', came into service with Bournemouth Fire Brigade in October 1929 and was its mainstay through the 1930s.

The Savoy Picture House in Boscombe (detail and with crowd) was destroyed by fire on 18 August 1930.

'Suffer little children to come unto me' was the theme of J. Suchomlin's sand sculpture on east beach, beside Bournemouth Pier, in 1931.

Columbia Road, between Wallisdown and Ensbury Park, typifying the new suburbia that came to Bournemouth with the parish of Kinson in the 1930s.

House on fire in Stewart Road, Charminster, in 1938.

PLJ 356, a Leyland dual-purpose fire engine, joined Bournemouth Fire Brigade in December 1939.

6: FIGHTING FORTIES

The Phoney War ended, for Britain and Bournemouth, at Dunkirk in May 1940. Following the fall of France, refugees crowded the town, along with thousands of French and United Kingdom soldiers who needed to recuperate before being re-formed and retrained. The country's one and only fully-equipped division was Canadian. Because of the scale of the threat, as the Battle of Britain followed in the summer of 1940, Bournemouth and the entire Dorset coast became 'military control areas' with artillery emplacements, pillboxes for machine-guns, anti-tank obstacles, urban 'defended boxes', beach defences and tens of thousands of mines.

The first visual casualties were the piers at both Bournemouth and Boscombe which were blown up by the Royal Engineers, leaving their seaward ends as derelict islands. My father used timbers from Bournemouth Pier in building our air-raid shelter beneath the garden shed in Easter Road. Destruction of the piers remained a gripe for Bournemouth hoteliers and traders for another decade and a half. Many other seaside towns had their piers left intact – but they had not been earmarked as destinations for Hitler's Operation Sealion.

General Sir Alan Brooke took over Southern Command and was less than impressed at the state of the Dorset defences. He confided to his diary on 2 July 1940:

> *The more I see of the nakedness of our defences the more appalled I am. Untrained men, no arms, no transport, and no equipment, And yet there are masses of men in uniform in this country, but they are mostly untrained, why I cannot think after ten months of war. The ghastly part of it is that I feel certain that we can only have a few more weeks before the Bosch attacks.*

Prime Minister Winston Churchill, who had taken over from Neville Chamberlain when Hitler's Panzers rolled into the Low Countries, saw things for himself on 17 July 1940. In between laying bricks and staring out to sea he recalled to Alan Brooke that he had passed the spot where, as a seventeen-year-old staying in Lady Wimborne's villa

at Branksome Dene, he had fallen from a rustic bridge while playing with his cousins in 1892. He had been unconscious for days and there had been fears for his life. The next day Brooke returned to Bournemouth and discussed an anti-invasion exercise with Major-General Bernard Montgomery.

Allied fighter pilots who were shot down over Bournemouth crashed into the sea, with the exception of Pilot Officer Cecil Hight, a New Zealander in a Spitfire of 234 Squadron. He fell to his death in Mr and Mrs Alfred Hoare's garden at Hambledon, Leven Avenue, on 17 August 1940. The Hoares were visited again by the war when Hambledon was hit by a bomb. The rescuers included the vicar of St Peter's, Canon Hedley Burrows, who recalled that 'the dear old man, Mr Hoare, died'. In the rubble he heard Mrs Hoare. She asked who it was. He replied and told her to keep still. 'Canon Burrows,' she said, 'how kind of you to come and see me today.'

Bournemouth received many visits from the Luftwaffe. The most terrifying was to Bourne Valley Gasworks at lunchtime on 27 March 1941 when a bomb hit the canteen and protruded through the ceiling, as workmen fled for the door, before it exploded. A total of 31 employees and three Home Guard soldiers were killed, and a further 23 people wounded. They were dragged from the debris by ARP wardens and Royal Artillerymen who struggled to prise them from a precarious lattice of overlapping girders and timber.

Alma Road Schools were left as a bomb-site into the next decade. Woolworths, on the west side of the Square at the foot of Commercial Road, was burnt out by an incendiary device at midnight on 10 April 1941. The same raider dropped a bomb which destroyed a flat in St Stephen's Road, killing the town's poet, Cumberland Clark. A white-haired gentleman with a walrus moustache he had produced the uplifting *War Songs of the Allies* which ironically contained his own exit line:

> *Let the bombs bounce round above us,*
> *And the shells come whizzing by,*
> *Down in our air-raid shelter*
> *We'll be cosy, you and I.*

Street Fire Fighting Parties were formed in 1941 and there was special emphasis on 'Dealing with incendiary bombs AT ONCE'. King George VI and Queen Elizabeth visited Bournemouth on 23 October 1941 to inspect Dominion airmen in the Pavilion. It was the town's first visit by a reigning sovereign.

Though blown off his bicycle as two bombs exploded either side of Southcote Road on 6 June 1942, ten-year-old Stewart Garrett jumped up and dusted himself down. An evacuee from Southampton – to escape the blitz – he lived in a three-storey billet which had been requisitioned in Derby Road. There his sister continued playing the piano as broken glass was held in place by a net curtain, which had been glazed to the window, as an air-raid precaution. Later that Saturday, Stewart and his mother found a metal cylinder, beneath broken branches in Kynveton Gardens. This turned out to the axle from a goods wagon in marshalling yards on the other side of Southcote Road. It had been blown over the rooftops by the force of the explosion. Just one of the bombs from Messerschmitt Me110 fighter-bombers had hit their target, the railway yards, but a total of 454 properties were damaged.

Lindbergh Road, a short street a stone's throw from Castle Lane in the suburb of Moordown, lost its name as a result of the war. It had been chosen as a tribute to the pioneer aviator Colonel Charles Augustus Lindbergh whose *Spirit of St Louis* made the first solo non-stop crossing of the Atlantic in 1927. By January 1943, the memory had soured, with Lindbergh expressing pro-Nazi sentiments. Bournemouth town councillors therefore decided to rename it Franklin Road – honouring the United States President, Franklin Delano Roosevelt.

Fifteen years later I met a man who returned to the home of my aunt and uncle, Effie and Frank Watts in the Grove at Moordown, where he lodged during the war. He told me he had worked in what was now a cosmetics factory but kept his lips sealed about the top-secret project. That reached its climax on the night of 30 January 1943 when Bomber Command used H2S airborne radar sets, operationally, for the first time. They were deployed in a raid over Hamburg and enabled Pathfinder flares to be dropped on their target.

The need for this apparatus had been apparent since the night of 9 March 1942 when Bomber Command, in its Chief's words, 'attacked Hamborn in mistake for Essen'. Sir Arthur Harris, Commander-in-Chief

Bomber Command, enthusiastically backed the development of H2S – promised for the previous autumn – which took its name from the chemical formula for the obnoxious gas hydrogen sulphide, because Churchill's chief scientific adviser, Professor Frederick Lindemann, hearing of it from the Telecommunication Research Establishment in the Isle of Purbeck, said, 'It stinks that we haven't thought of it before!'

The invention was made by Group 8, working from a Nissen hut in the grounds of the Establishment's eastern out-station, Leeson House, at Langton Matravers. 'TF' was its earlier code but this was reckoned to be a give-away – try for yourself and check below – and it came into being after J.T. Randall and H.A.H. Boot invented the centrimetric valve which was put into the new Beaufighter. Giving power on a low wavelength it provided an image on a screen that showed features of the ground below. This was initially tested by a Blenheim bomber at 8000 feet above the Air Defence Establishment beside Christchurch Aerodrome. Houses of Christchurch and Bournemouth could be distinguished from the adjoining heathland and meadows.

Six more flights were made and then Halifax bomber V9977 was drafted to the new aerodrome at RAF Hurn for fitting with the first specially designed unit shielded in a cupola protruding from the belly, which made the aeroplane seem ungainly and pregnant. The casing was perspex. Bomber V9977 would be lost, along with the inventor of Airborne Interception radar, thirty-eight-year-old Alan Blumlein, in a test flight from RAF Defford on 7 June 1942. Air Commodore Donald 'Pathfinder' Bennett tried the apparatus with the result that Winston Churchill agreed it should be in production by the end of 1942. The Prototype Research Unit made the sets – which were perfected by Philip Gee and Bernard Lovell at Worth Matravers – in a factory beside Northbourne Golf Links at West Howe, Bournemouth.

The earlier codename 'TF' stood for 'Town Finder'. The factory at West Howe that produced H2S later made real smells for cosmetics company Max Factor.

In practice, H2S was to create its own disaster, as the Germans realised that not only could it be jammed but that advanced technology would enable exploitation of the signals. Luftwaffe fighters began to find their targets by homing in upon waveforms radiating from the bombers. This again accelerated the rate of losses. On 30 March 1944 a total of 94 British bombers were shot down in a night raid on Nuremberg and of those that made it home 71 were damaged.

Even as wartime operations turned from defensive into offensive, Bournemouth continued to see and suffer front-line attacks, such as the naval battle that was clearly visible from the cliffs on 8 March 1943. German E-boats failed to ambush a coastal convoy off Devon and escaped eastwards, pursued by the Polish destroyer *Krakowaik* until she had to pull into Poole to refuel. Six-inch coast defence batteries then opened up from Brownsea Island, Hengistbury Head, and Mudeford, aided by 3.7-inch dual anti-air and anti-ship emplacements and the 40-mm Bofors anti-aircraft guns along the Bournemouth cliffs.

There were German losses in Poole Bay. Two bodies and four survivors were brought to Mudeford Quay by the picket-boat *Robert T. Hillary*. This former lifeboat was crewed by the Royal Navy Volunteer Reserve.

During March 1943 children visiting the aviaries in the Pleasure Gardens at Bournemouth found themselves watching the rabbits. Gone were most of the exotic birds of the jungle for which these cages had been renowned. Parks department staff began supplying bunnies to British Restaurants where rabbit pie was added to the menu.

Likewise, throughout the suburbs, animal husbandry took over when the tedium of spade-work caused relapse into boredom for those who only reluctantly responded to C. H. Middleton's 'Dig for Victory' exhortations in his famous wireless broadcasts. Chicken, bantams and even the occasional pig rooted around beneath rabbit hutches. Postwar survivors became our pets in the 1950s.

From cock-crow onwards Bournemouth resonated with sounds of the farmyard. There was also a revival of the Victorian allotment movement. Gardeners took over open spaces and potential building sites and here, at least, Mr Middleton's words were heeded:

These are critical times, but we shall get through them, and the harder we dig for victory the sooner will the roses be with us again.

Tiring of the usual pranks, such as swapping over householders' gates and front-door mats, some Bournemouth-bound schoolboys played a more contemporary wheeze on their mates for April Fools' Day in 1943.

They spread the rumour around the bus that sweets and chocolates had been removed from the food ration and would no longer require coupons. 'I bet dozens of chaps will run into the shops,' said the joker. He was proved correct. Rationing continued for another decade, until after Churchill returned as Prime Minister, and insisted upon its abolition in time for the coronation of Queen Elizabeth II.

Sunday 23 May 1943 was the worst day in Bournemouth's history. At lunchtime, within five minutes of 13.00 hours, more than a hundred people were killed and dozens of buildings were left in ruins. Beales department store became a burnt-out shell. West's Picture House in the former Shaftesbury Hall in Old Christchurch Road was destroyed. The Central Hotel in the Square fell apart. Facing it the drapers Bobby & Co. Ltd had a frontage shattered by blast damage. The omnibus standing area beside the Bus Station in Exeter Road was covered in glass from 25 Hants & Dorset buses that lost all their windows. Punshon Memorial Church, on Richmond Hill, was ripped apart. The Metropole Hotel at the Lansdowne also collapsed. The Shamrock and Rambler coach depot in Holdenhurst Road was devastated.

Bombs also fell into residential areas at Bethia Road, Cotlands Road, Dean Park Road, Drummond Road, Howeth Road, Lansdowne Road, Vale Road, Queen's Park South Drive, and between Pokesdown and Iford Bridge. Of the 3481 buildings that were damaged about 40 had to be demolished.

Seventy-seven civilians were dead and the bodies of 24 Empire airmen and other military personnel were recovered from the debris of the Metropole Hotel. Firemen of National Fire Service, with a new 100-feet turntable ladder, rescued a further 35 airmen who were trapped on the upper floors of the elegant Victorian building, dating from 1893, which occupied the triangular corner between Holdenhurst Road and Christchurch Road. A total of 196 people were treated for their injuries.

The attack came when 22 Focke-Wulf FW190s swept in low from the sea and bombed the central shopping areas of the Square and Lansdowne. But for the fact that the attack coincided with Sunday lunchtime the casualty figures could have been much higher.

Two hours later the conductor of the BBC Orchestra, Sir Adrian Boult, took the Bournemouth Municipal Orchestra through the Nimrod passage from Sir Edward Elgar's *Enigma Variations* in memory of those who had died. The bombs marred what had been intended as a celebratory concert to mark the 50th anniversary of the Bournemouth Orchestra.

Meanwhile, at 14.20 hours, Bournemouth ARP Control Centre requested rescue parties from Christchurch and Poole. A major fire was still burning around Beales, where the bombs fractured a gas main, and at one time threatened the adjoining department store of J.J. Allen and St Peter's Church. Pumping parties dragged multiple snakes of hoses to the Bourne Stream to supplement the reservoir-fed gutter-laid pavement-level network of the emergency on-ground water supply. Others formed a chain to pass buckets of water up the slope.

It was not only the concert that proceeded as planned. Windowless buses went back into service during the afternoon with sacks tied across the front of the vehicles to reduce draughts.

Five of the FW190s were reportedly shot down. One crashed beside St Ives Hotel, at 34 Grove Road, with an unexploded bomb still attached. The pilot, Unteroffizier F.K. Schmidt, was killed. Though the bomb failed to explode, the aircraft caught fire and the hotel was gutted. Another fighter was seen to crash in the bay and was credited to a machine-gun post of the 87th Light Anti-Aircraft Regiment of the Royal Artillery which was emplaced on the former flat roof of J.E. Beale Ltd. Its triple Lewis guns were manned by Lance-Bombadier John Howard and Lance-Bombadier Norman Lawrence. RAF figures later showed that the five destruction claims against the FW190s were overstated. Two had been destroyed, as described, and two more were damaged.

Falling masonry later killed one of the men who finished the demolition of Beales. The principal buildings would remain as bomb sites for more than a decade. West's Picture House is now the Burlington Arcade. Beales was replaced and Bobby's repaired. Other lost landmarks became building sites for shops and offices.

The next significant raid came at 01.10 hours on 12 August 1943 when gas mains were set alight, water pipes fractured, and 1455 properties damaged as eight high-explosive bombs dropped on Bournemouth. Thirteen people were killed and 21

received hospital treatment. The bombs fell at the corner of Firs Glen Road and Woods View Road; at the junction of Boundary Road with Beswick Road; at the corner of Wilton Road and Gloucester Road; in Spring Road; Charminster Avenue; and Shelbourne Road.

A total of 23 high-explosive bombs fell on Bournemouth at teatime on 1 November 1943. The raid took place at 17.45 hours and left 1284 properties damaged. The casualty toll, however, was light, with just one person killed and 27 injured. Widespread damage was reported from Cecil Avenue, Howard Road, Campbell Road, Borthwick Road, Avon Road, Chatsworth Road, Bennett Road, Orcheston Road, Shaftesbury Road, and Shelbourne Road. Bombs at Queen's Park Avenue did little more than crater the golf links.

Lord Brabazon, the former Minister of Aircraft Production, was the principal speaker at a ceremony in the Town Hall on 17 December 1943, to present a plaque and certificate of merit on behalf of the National Savings Campaign. The town collected £2,033,894 in the 'Wings for Victory' week, held in May that year.

The award of the plaque was made by Group Captain Hutchinson of the Royal Canadian Air Force. Councillors and collectors were told that the money had been invested in a flight of six Sunderland flying-boats; three squadrons of 15 single-engine fighters; three squadrons of 12 four-engine bombers; plus three two-engine bombers:

'That is a grand total of 90 aircraft – at an average price of £22,598 each. Well done Bournemouth!'

As Dorset became an armed camp for 80,000 United States soldiers and their equipment, in December 1943, there was excitement at Longham when a heavy tank skidded off the road and careered into the public bar of the King's Arms Inn. The side of the building would have collapsed but for the turret of the tank which ended up supporting the bedroom floor and the bed of Michael Weaver, recovering from a bout of influenza. He was the son of landlord Leslie Weaver. One soldier in the tank was slightly hurt but all the occupants of the bar, in the process of leaving at closing time, had remarkable escapes.

The build-up was for the invasion of Europe though every effort was made to persuade the enemy that the offensive would actually come much further to the east between the Seine and the Pas de Calais. Plans for the actual assaults, in Normandy, also changed as Dorset was allocated to American Force O for Omaha and British Force G for Gold found its departure point centred on Southampton. Both armies came under the command of General Dwight D. Eisenhower, as Supreme Commander, with General Sir Bernard Montgomery as his operational land-force commander.

They stayed at the Carlton Hotel in February 1944 and discussed tactics. Major rehearsals included the live-firing Exercise Smash – visible across the bay on Tuesday 18 April 1944 – in which assault landings took place on Studland beach, as the perfect match for the sands of Normandy. King George VI stayed the previous night at the Hotel Grosvenor in Swanage and was woken at 04.00 hours to take up his binoculars, behind 3 feet of protective concrete in Fort Henry observation post, and watch landing craft coming ashore with the tide at dawn. Mines, shells, rockets and bombs gave added realism whilst American anti-aircraft artillery was in place in case the Luftwaffe turned up.

The sky was now full of Allied aircraft. Thunderbolt fighter-bombers of United States Army Air Force from Christchurch and RAF Typhoons from Hurn crossed the Channel to hit strategic targets and 'anything that moves' in Normandy and Britanny. Air defence was provided by Mosquito night-fighters. Four-engined Halifax bombers towed Horsa or Hamilcar troop-carrying gliders in a seemingly perpetual series of exercises with airborne forces. One of these Halifax tug-planes went into the sea beside Bournemouth Pier on 22 January 1944 and another Halifax bomber crashed at Moordown.

Heavily-laden JP137 from RAF Hurn took off on a delivery flight, for North Africa, just after midnight. It failed to gain sufficient height to cross the 120-feet high Bournemouth plateau. Minutes later, at 00.35 hours on 12 March 1944, it clipped the roofs of Willis builders' merchants and the former tram-depot beside Wimborne Road. Then it bounded off the roof of a house in Malvern Road and went into a ricochet above the home of Mr and Mrs Claw before finally diving into the ground beside the garage to Meadow Court. Both wings were ripped off and the corner of the main building was hit, killing Mrs D. Bennett in flat No. 9.

The fuselage and tail rolled over on to the back wash-houses, behind two pairs of Victorian cottages, next to the flats. Percy Chislett was killed in the centre cottage, at No. 1027 Wimborne Road, but his wife and teenage son were able to escape from an inferno of exploding ammunition by scrambling out of the front bedroom window. The pilot, Sgt Dennis Evans, and his six-man crew were killed.

This was the first Bournemouth war-story to be imparted to me as a child, with the questions having been triggered by the advertising hoardings beside the main road, across the sites of a couple of demolished houses. My other memory from Malvern Road was that one of the older buildings had discoloured windows. This was 'oiled glass' – as my father called it – which had been caused by a chemical reaction to the explosion. It struck me at the time that these were like photographs of the blast.

After the greatest sea and air armada in history, on 6 June 1944, the war was taken from Devon, Dorset and Hampshire to the mainland of Europe and moved gradually eastwards towards the Reich. To me the most significant relic of Bournemouth's war is the site of the pyrotechnics of the 'Major Strategic Night Decoy' in the pinewoods at the western end of Brownsea Island. This attracted a total of 1000 tons of German bombs which would otherwise have fallen on the Bournemouth conurbation. I can declare a personal interest in this because had they found their target then there would have been a high chance that I would never have been born.

The adrenalin of war was followed by that of a sensational double-murder case. Psychopath Neville Heath (1917–46) carried out a sex killing in Notting Hill and then came to Bournemouth where he booked into the Tollard Royal Hotel under an assumed name and rank that were hardly going to pass without comment. The handsome and debonair Group Captain Rupert Brooke, as he called himself, entertained Miss Doreen Marshall. Her body was found dumped in rhododendron bushes at Branksome Dene Chine on 3 July 1946. Neville Heath stood trial at the Old Bailey and was hanged on 26 September 1946.

The mines were removed from the beach, but much of it had been washed away during the conflict, and the dismantled piers presented a sad sight. Despite this, Bournemouth Pier was back in business, at 11.00 hours on 17 August 1946. A temporary wooden gangway linked the stumps and 'island' with the entrance and the Red Funnel steamer *Princess Elizabeth* came alongside from

Southampton. She brought 600 passengers and cast-off again that Saturday afternoon, on a trip across the bay, to Swanage.

Three weeks later there was an echo from the war as a mine, missed by the clearance team, was washed out of the cliff and exploded at Southbourne. Bournemouth Pier was properly re-bridged in April 1947, with buildings at the end being rebuilt in April 1950, but Boscombe Pier languished in limbo for another decade until its reopening in 1960.

Professional football resumed in 1946 with Boscombe Football Club – the Cherries – winning against Walsall in the Football League. In 1947, Bournemouth traders were outraged when they heard that the Bournemouth Municipal Orchestra would be conducted by Austrian-born Rudolf Schwarz (1905–94) who had been musical director of the Jewish Cultural Organisation in Berlin from 1936 until its closure by the Gestapo in 1941. A year later he was taken to a concentration camp and weighed less than seven stones when he was liberated by British troops from infamous Belsen in 1945. One of the Bournemouth councillors tried to defend his appointment:

Nothing debarred Sir Henry Wood or Sir Thomas Beecham from applying.

Unfortunately this became a national joke – as Sir Henry Wood had died in 1944 – and the town was held up to ridicule by a spoof letter in the satirical Beachcomber column of the *Daily Express*:

Sir, Rather than see a foreigner in charge of Bournemouth's music, I would have the Municipal Orchestra composed of substantial tradesmen without a note of music in them, with a citizen of standing to conduct – perhaps the Mayor himself. This would not be, musically speaking, the best orchestra, but it would be British to the core, and an advertisement to tourists that we know our own minds.

Yours faithfully,
MUSIC LOVER.

The 5th Battalion, the Northamptonshire Regiment, on manoeuvres through Holdenhurst Farm in 1940.

The 12th Battalion, the Hampshire Regiment, attacking Bournemouth cliffs in an exercise in 1940.

New Zealand Pilot Officer Cecil Hight who fell to his death from a Spitfire over Leven Avenue on 17 August 1940.

Poet Cumberland Clark, seen on Bournemouth Pier, died when his flat in St Stephen's Road was hit by a bomb at midnight on 10 April 1941.

The Hotel Metropole, between Holdenhurst Road and Christchurch Road at the Lansdowne, was the greatest and most tragic of Bournemouth's war losses.

There were dozens of Canadian casualties when the Metropole Hotel received a direct hit in the town's lunchtime attack on 23 May 1943.

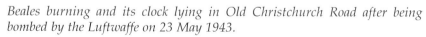

Beales burning and its clock lying in Old Christchurch Road after being bombed by the Luftwaffe on 23 May 1943.

Sir Adrian Boult conducting the golden jubilee concert of Bournemouth Municipal Orchestra on 23 May 1943, two hours after it had become the town's saddest day.

Supreme Allied Commander Dwight D. Eisenhower (left) and his top land-force officer, General Sir Bernard Montgomery, working on D-Day invasion plans at the Carlton Hotel in the spring of 1944.

Bournemouth's wartime fire-women, from division 16-C of the National Fire Brigade, marching in a Victory Parade, 1945.

Ted Legg, the author's father, outside his shoe shop on Peters Hill in Wimborne Road, Winton.

Father Ted Legg and son Rodney, whose joint memories and photographic collection form the basis of this book, in their garden at Easter Road, Moordown, in December 1949.

7: FRAUGHT FIFTIES

Artistically, the Bournemouth Municipal Orchestra flourished under the baton of Rudolf Schwarz, and he took them through Elgar's First Symphony on 25 May 1950. Three days later they become the first British symphony orchestra to strike. The Musicians' Union had called out its Bournemouth members because of a dispute over another group of musicians – Ted Green's military band in Pine Walk – who they argued were being underpaid. The union eventually backed down and concerts resumed at the end of July 1950.

The aide-de-camp to the new Queen in 1952 was Bournemouth-born Rear-Admiral Sir Edward Rebbeck (1901–83). He had served in the First World War in HMS *Erin* and in the Second World War in HMS *Birmingham*, before making his mark in naval aviation, finishing his career in command of the Navy's reserve aircraft.

The actress Dame Sybil Thorndike (1882–1976) lived for many years at Kinson House beside Wimborne Road. She was the wife of theatre producer Sir Lewis Casson (1875–1969). Their house and its grounds were cleared in the 1950s and replaced with blocks of flats.

Home entertainment was about to arrive on the scene. The first television in Easter Road, a tiny Bush set in the home of Mr and Mrs Reginald Sprague at No. 14, appeared in time for the coronation of Queen Elizabethan II in 1953. Roger Burridge, Norman Chislett, Douglas Dunning and I crossed the street and squeezed into the sitting room. My enduring first image, however, is of cowboys and Indians rather than Westminster Abbey or the conquest of Everest. Provision of our own sets was kept on hold until the advent of commercial television in 1957.

One Wednesday we lined up in the playground of Charminster Primary School to watch the partial eclipse of the sun, through candle-smoked glass negatives, as the lunar shadow rounded the earth. It was on 30 June 1954 and the closest point of total eclipse was the Shetland island of Unst but there the phenomenon was spoilt by bad weather. The lights were also going out across the British Empire.

In the hiatus between Churchill's final administration and the coming crisis over the Egyptian nationalisation of the Suez Canal, Prime Minister Sir Anthony Eden brought the Conservative Party Conference to Bournemouth. They booked into the Carlton Hotel on 7 October 1955. In the hotel register, the signature of journalist Henry Fairlie is followed by those of the Downing Street entourage. There follows the Duke of Wellington from Stratfield Saye, and the Earl and Countess of Shaftesbury from St Giles House, who had welcomed them on behalf of the Hampshire and Dorset aristocracy.

They saw the mix of postwar dereliction and recovery that was the Bournemouth of my childhood. The Chancellor of the Exchequer between 1951 and 1955 was Richard Austen Butler. Rab, as I kept hearing for another three decades, was 'the best Prime Minister we never had'. They had a nice anecdote about him at the Carlton, concerning a request to a receptionist for writing paper and envelopes, most of which he then handed back:

Thank you, young lady, but in the job I do at the moment I don't have that number of friends.

Arthur Frederick Daubeney Olav Eveleigh-de-Moleyns, 7th Baron Ventry (1898–1987) was Britain's leading postwar expert on airships. He lived at Lindsay Hall in Lindsay Road and named his greatest creation after his adopted town. *Bournemouth*, however, hardly lifted any higher than the open-top yellow bus to which she was tethered on 19 July 1951. Briefly breaking loose from her mooring she came to an ignominious end on the gymnasium roof of RAF Cardington.

Few shed any tears. Stories and pictures of pre-war airships as balls of fire with falling bodies were disaster images of that time. *Bournemouth*, though minuscule in comparison, was the first British airship since the *R101* left the same great hangar at Cardington, Bedfordshire, on 5 October 1930 and came to grief at Beauvais, France. Among the 48 people who died then was Lord Thompson, the Secretary of State for Air, and Major-General Sir Sefton Brancker, Director of Civil Aviation. It was hardly conducive to winning official support for such projects.

More enthusiasm, however, was shown for the flight as far as Bournemouth of the prototype Bristol Brabazon, named for Lord Brabazon of Tara – wartime Minister of Aircraft Production – who in 1909 was the first resident Briton to make an officially recognised aeroplane flight in the British Isles. The great airliner had taken off from Filton, Bristol, and word reached us it was heading for Hurn. We watched from waste ground on the corner of Malvern Road and Homeside Road as she turned for home over the Stour valley. You needed both hands to count the engines. No one had ever seen that number of propellers. Unbeknown to us, they were shaking the airframe apart, and the project was scrapped.

Local newspapers never ceased to remind us that the boxer Freddie Mills (1919–65) was born in Terrace Road. He entered boxing in 1935 and went all the way to the top, becoming world light-heavy-weight champion, in 1948. By 1950 he was a London businessman, having opened the Freddie Mills Nite Spot, at Charing Cross. His final headlines were a decade and a half later when he was found dead in a car behind his nightclub. A fairground rifle was propped beside him and there was a single bullet in his head. Though an inquest returned a suicide verdict, his family thought otherwise, claiming that he had been murdered by gangsters.

Town pride was also lifted by Boscombe Football Club, which reached the fourth round of the Football Association Cup in 1956. A Third Division team, they were away to Wolverhampton when Boscombe's Reg Cutler stopped the match for several minutes, after colliding with the Wolves goalpost with such force that it required immediate carpentry. Club players who went on to achieve a national reputation have included George Best, Colin Clarke, Charlie George and Mel Machin. Staying with the club for much longer, from 1956 to 1969, Ray Bumstead notched up a record of 412 Football League appearances.

Creator of a mythical and magical world, John Ronald Reuel Tolkien (1892–1973) spent his holidays at the Miramar Hotel, East Overcliff Drive, in the 1950s and '60s. Then he retired with his wife, Edith Bratt, to a bungalow at No. 19 Lakeside Road, Branksome Park. She died in 1971 and Tolkien returned to Oxford, where he had been a superb historian of the real world as Professor of Anglo-Saxon from 1925 until 1945 when he became Merton Professor of English Language and Literature.

It was in Oxford that his mind-children of *The Hobbit* and *The Lord of the Rings* were created and discussed at meetings of 'the Inklings' in the back bar of the Eagle and Child in St Giles. His cronies included C.S. Lewis and the poet and novelist Charles Williams. Theirs was an elitist but productive literary clique. Tolkien's death occurred in Bournemouth, when he came back to stay with his old friends Dr and Mrs D.A. Tolhurst, in Little Forest Road.

One of the last of the familiar bomb-sites became Bristol and West House in 1958 with the redevelopment of the gaping sites of Punshon Memorial Church and the Central Hotel on the corner of Richmond Hill and Post Office Road. That year also saw the demolition of Howe Lodge at Kinson which was of some notoriety as the home of smuggling godfather Isaac Gulliver who became a Wimborne banker and founded a financial dynasty.

It also laid the ghost of Oubee. A North American from the Beothuk tribe in Newfoundland, she was brought to Howe Lodge by Poole merchant Thomas Stone, in 1792. Her father had been shot dead when settlers attacked a Beothuk family in their wigwam. These were the original 'Red Indians' – they covered themselves and their possessions with red ochre – and Oubee was the informant who enabled a unique vocabulary to be compiled of what soon became a dead language. European disease finished off Oubee, apparently in 1795 from tuberculosis, to which she had no resistance. She is mentioned in the diary of Benjamin Lester, another Poole businessman with agents in Trinity, Newfoundland, but her burial place is unknown.

The home of the nuns of St Francis' Church in Court Road, Charminster, was hit by lightning in the late 1950s and a 'Million Pennies Appeal' (£4,166 13s. 4d.) was launched to rehouse them. Stretched out along the street the money would have reached to the Martyrs' Inn at Tolpuddle.

Theirs was not the only dramatic bolt from the heavens. Another split apart the house on the triangular corner plot between Evelyn Road and Coronation Avenue, Moordown, and left stairs and the chimney hanging in the sky. Castle Parade, between Muscliffe Road and the Castle Laundry in Castle Road, Winton, was blown apart by a gas explosion. This killed the kindly shopkeeper, who I presume was Alfred William Mitchell of grocers A.W. Mitchell, and I retain a last vision of him in his white coat, smiling across the counter, and benignly accepting a go-cart load of discarded bottles. I had collected these on the beach and trundled them inland – for their deposits – in desperation after town-centre traders who sold them refused to have them back.

I was usually relatively rich when I called on Mr Mitchell as it was our pit-stop before returning home to Easter Road after delivering cart-loads of newspapers and cardboard to waste-paper merchants W.A. Alexander & Son. Known to us as Powell's, they were in the heart of artisan suburbia, at No. 29 Muscliffe Road.

On another personal note, in 1958 a golfer at Queen's Park was silly enough to challenge this child's primacy as to the use of the parkland for air and exercise. In the next couple of years I hit back by running across the fairways and confiscating several hundred golf balls, some of which I sold back to golfers, but most of which I saw again one day as globules of molten rubber strewn across the black stubble of gorse-land beside the then unwidened Holdenhurst Road, following a heath fire.

More constructively, but with less result, I collected names protesting against Wessex Way inner relief road being built through the middle of Horseshoe Common, which despite the road is my favourite semi-wild haven of tranquillity in the town.

The town also had unexpected wildernesses, such as the roundabout island in the centre of the Square, where the vegetation was dense enough to conceal a tent full of French students for more than a week. I've been under there, literally, on a walk of the Bourne Stream, wading it in plimsolls from the Pier Approach up to and through the tunnel in the huge embankment at Bourne Valley. I managed to crawl through all the obstacles bar one set of culvert gratings which forced me to scurry overground at a road crossing. 'Creeping' was a more anti-social form of juvenile expedition which took place on winter nights when we crept out of bed and then over fences, with the objective of reaching back-gardens in one of the adjoining streets, which

were Malvern Road, Naseby Road and Limited Road. By the following evening the secret always seemed to be out.

Bournemouth maintains a plentiful supply of eccentrics. A stone's throw from Winton Secondary School for Boys – a distance we proved as fact – lived a lady who claimed direct descent from Queen Victoria and was distressed not to have been asked to meet the Archbishop of Canterbury in Westminster Abbey. I would like to do justice to her claim but I have combined and confused her diatribes with those of two other similarly dressed ladies, to whom I delivered milk on a Saturday round. Every other week they would collect the dregs of a whole fortnight's bottles and hand me for replacement a three-quarters full bottle – contents virtually green – claiming it was 'delivered yesterday and has gone off'.

More interesting, in terms of a potted biography, was self-confessed witch Doreen Valiente (1922–99), regarded by many as the 'Earth Mother' of modern paganism, who discarded her broomstick in childhood but believed all her life that the physical world was merely a 'painted veil'. While living in Bournemouth at the time of the repeal of the last Witchcraft Act, in 1951, Doreen Dominey and husband Casimiro Valiente were introduced to fertility rituals by Gerald Gardner. She was initiated as a witch at a midsummer ceremony in 1953, with rites conducted in the nude, and accompanied by ritual scourging. Her version of the induction, published as *Charge of the Goddess*, is now recited by pagans worldwide.

She proceeded to publish a series of books to publicise the craft – arguing that its survival depended upon finding a new generation of recruits – and hosted the inaugural dinner of the Witchcraft Research Association in 1964. This was followed by an unprecedented 1500 attendance at a Pagan Federation Conference, in 1977, at which she urged 'a regenerated and enlightened paganism' in which all could partake in 'uninhibited sexual enjoyment'. To her dying day she believed that Margaret Thatcher was the reincarnation of Queen Elizabeth I, which could explain a lot, including the famous phrase 'we are a grandmother'.

Bournemouth, *emerging from a huge hangar at Cardington, Bedfordshire, was Britain's first airship since the pre-war R101 disaster.*

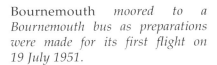

Bournemouth *moored to a Bournemouth bus as preparations were made for its first flight on 19 July 1951.*

Airborne, technically at least, Bournemouth *just managed to cross a road.*

Lord Ventry's high hopes for lighter-than-air flight ended on a Cardington rooftop.

Coronation line-up at Charminster Infants School in 1953 with author Rodney Legg looking particularly patriotic.

Westwards from Bournemouth Corporation Baths, across Pier Approach, to the boarding houses of Southcliff Road.

Postwar youngsters liberated Children's Corner in the Lower Gardens and took to the water during a series of hot summers.

Alum Chine Tea-Rooms and the beach as it used to look, with a north wind billowing the deckchairs earlier in the century, before the building of the promenade.

'Use Private Enterprise' was the slogan over Alum Chine Tea-Rooms (bottom left) in the 1950s, with 'Sand Trays Served Here' (foreground).

Guns were for play in the 1950s with Norman Chislett (left) and Rodney Legg defending a water-butt in Easter Road.

Howe Lodge at Kinson, the last house from smuggling days, was demolished in 1958.

8: SWINGING SIXTIES

The decade opened with a murder hunt, after the body of mother-of-four Mrs Lilian Thorne from Alder Road was found dumped in Wheelers Lane, beside Northbourne Golf Course on 17 January 1960. The site of the grim discovery was in fact one that we boys had cycled past the previous afternoon – a Sunday – thus narrowly missing being the ones to find the body. Murders in those days were not only rarer but still carried the added twist of a potential sequel for the perpetrator, at the end of the hangman's rope.

The population was still rising, to 155,000, and ageing in its demographic profile as new estates of bungalows attracted increasing numbers of retired incomers. Trolley-buses were on their way out. In one of the most retrograde moves ever inflicted upon successful public transport, the electric powered vehicles with their overhead wires – and the assurance of fixed, reliable routes – were replaced by particulate-disgorging diesel buses. They offered a certain flexibility but at the cost of removing the assurance and certainty of the old routes. Passenger numbers may have been declining but now they slid.

The sixties also saw the de-industrialisation of Bournemouth. The old potteries were closing from Parkstone and Branksome to West Howe and Kinson. One of the old landmarks was Elliott's brickworks, at Bear Cross, established between 1880 and 1900. It had already moved southwards, to the higher end of Poole Lane, when the clay seam was exhausted. There, as Elliott's Pottery, it extended its range of terracotta ware, roof tiles, fire-bricks and stoneware drain pipes. The business closed in 1966.

That year Bournemouth had royal visitors. Queen Elizabeth II and the Duke of Edinburgh were in Wimborne Road on 15 July 1966 to recognise the work of the Centre for the Residential Care of Young Men suffering from Muscular Dystrophy. They went on to Town Hall and King's Park where the Mayor, Alderman Philip Whitelegg, walked on the grass as he accompanied Her Majesty along the red carpet to a commemorative tree that awaited beside the entrance to the Athletic Centre.

The railways faced major change. After Dr Richard Beeching's report, branch lines into Bournemouth from Bath and Salisbury were condemned to closure. Their terminus, Bournemouth West Station beside the Queen's Hotel at Westbourne, saw its last rail travellers on 3 October 1965 and is now beneath Wessex Way. It had brought generations of northern visitors to the coast on the Pines Express from Birmingham and Manchester, which was diverted to Poole until ceasing on 4 March 1967. It was later briefly reinstated as a name but was finally abandoned in June 2002.

The last main-line steam services in Britain continued between Bournemouth and Waterloo until the laying of continuous-welded track and resignalling enabled electrification to begin on 10 July 1967. The final 256 steam engines on Southern Region of British Railways followed their predecessors to the scrapyard though many of those that arrived at Barry Dock were rescued for use on private lines.

Chess players on Bournemouth Pier.

The seven-storey replacement for Beales department store in Old Christchurch Road which was destroyed by wartime bombs.

'Bingo' as the Moderne Cinema in Wimborne Road, Moordown, moved with the times in the 1960s.

Queen Elizabeth II, with Mayor Philip Whitelegg, after planting a tree in King's Park on 15 July 1966.

Elliott's Pottery, in the brick-fields between Turbury Common and West Howe, was the last of Bournemouth old industries in the 1950s.

Southern Region locomotive No. 2038 steaming out of Bournemouth Central Station, with an up-train, beside the Post Office sorting office (top right).

The dying days of steam, after removal of the middle tracks in the 1960s (foreground), with an unwashed up-train taking on water at Bournemouth Central Station.

Steam engine No. 75077 emerging with a down-train from underneath Holdenhurst Road, below the South Western Hotel (left).

Ursula (right) and sister Pullman coaches of the Bournemouth Belle *coming out of the sidings northwest of Bournemouth Central Station in the 1960s.*

Locomotives Nos 41224 and 73020 (centre) heading into the maintenance depot northwest of the Central Station.

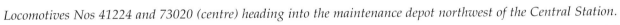

Pit-stop for No. 34024 and an oiling for No. 35007 in the train-care yard beside the Central Station.

The track towards Poole (right) out of Bournemouth Central Station (top left).

One of the last steam trains to Weymouth, seen after removal of the middle track (foreground), beside the down-platform at Bournemouth Central Station.

The northwest side of Bournemouth Central Station in 1970, southwestwards to St Paul's Church (centre).

9: SETTLED SEVENTIES

For an eighteen-year-old holidaymaker from Hemel Hempstead, there was a painful reminder of a secret danger lurking beneath Bournemouth's golden sands. Weaver fish work their way into the sand at the low-tide mark and are most plentiful in late summer. These little creatures can inflict an intense sting from a row of sharp black spines along their backs. Linda Dargue victim of a weaver fish, on 29 August 1974, left hospital after treatment.

Poole Council's contribution to the opening of European Architectural Heritage Year in 1975 was marked by the demolition of the historic lodge at County Gates. 'This cottage, designed by William Burn and built in the 1850s, was the last remaining link with the Branksome Towers Estate,' said Leigh Hatts of Bournemouth Civic Society. The lodge stood at the Westbourne entrance to The Avenue, which was the former driveway to Branksome Tower. This house had been the setting for Edgar Wallace's *Mr Justice Maxwell*, which was published in 1922. 'It appears that almost every link with Wallace has been destroyed in time for his centenary this April,' Mr Hatts sighed.

Perhaps the most unlikely son of Bournemouth was the tycoon Harold S. Geneen. We heard about him repeatedly through the seventies, usually with the reminder that he was born 'improbably enough' in Bournemouth, apparently around 1910. The uncertainty was caused by the fact that Hal Geneen was in England for only a year before his Russian father and Italian-born mother left for America. He was devoted to his mother, who brought him up in Connecticut after her marriage failed, and he has commemorated her in London with a teak bench in the gardens opposite the Connaught Hotel:

In Memory of Aida Geneen, who loved the gardens of her native England, from her son Harold S. Geneen.

By 1972, having turned ITT [International Telephone and Telegraph] into a global giant, he had pledged $400,000 towards the San Diego Republican Party convention and Richard Nixon's return to the White House. What propelled him into scandal and was to be instrumental in bringing Nixon down after the Watergate break-in, was a secret memo, published by Washington columnist Jack Anderson, with the hand-written note: 'Please destroy this, huh?'

The recipient failed to do so. Its crucial contribution to world history was to implicate President Nixon, Attorney-General John Mitchell and henchmen Ed Reinecke and Bob Haldeman in a conspiratorial fix of an anti-trust case against ITT. Lobbyist Mrs Dita Beard, writing to ITT's Washington chief Bill Merriam, had disclosed that 'our noble commitment has gone a long way toward our negotiations on mergers eventually coming out as Hal wants them … we all know Hal and his big mouth'.

Footbridge across the site of Holloway's Dock, from which ironstone had been exported from Hengistbury Head.

Debenhams (top left) and Woolworths (centre), rebuilt after wartime bombing, in a view westwards across the Square roundabout to Commercial Road, in 1975.

10: ENLIGHTENED EIGHTIES

In 1980, for the first time in more than a hundred years, it was no longer possible to see the national and regional newspapers at a public reading room in Bournemouth. A service that the Victorians took for granted was targeted by the latest spending curbs. There was no longer anywhere within 50 miles where you could monitor all the national press and it left the racks almost empty on the first floor of the Central Library at the Lansdowne. The only survivors, apart from a handful of local papers, were the *Guardian*, *Daily Telegraph*, and *The Times*.

Over the years the coverage had already been gradually reduced – helped by closures as Fleet Street shrank – and the latest cancellations were for 'all the tabloids and provincial newspapers'. The latter included the *Western Morning News* from Plymouth, the *Western Daily Press* from Bristol, the *Western Mail* from Cardiff, the *Birmingham Post*, *Liverpool Echo*, *Yorkshire Post*, *The Scotsman* and *Glasgow Herald*. For me it was the end of an era – such a sad life I have led – as I used to cycle there every Saturday morning to read the papers. A similar process of attrition was taking its toll of magazines and journals. Electrical words and images would soon replace the printed versions.

The physical shape of the future was taking to the sky on the edge of the West Cliff in Exeter Road. The site of Darwin's Cliff Cottage had been replaced by a pair of apartment blocks in 1876, which were merged into Southcliff Tower, and became the Regent Palace Hotel. This was demolished in 1981 and the site became the key to Bournemouth's destiny.

Building work through 1982 saw the creation of a 4000-seat hall plus another smaller one for 1200 delegates in a huge multi-purpose conference and leisure centre. It also incorporates a swimming pool and restaurants. The building was seen as a way to extend the town's visitor months into October's party political conference season and to sustain the resort's crucial tourist income. That, at the time, was estimated at £150 million a year.

The BIC – Bournemouth International Centre – was soon putting Bournemouth first with the news on national television but the Winter Gardens still

played its part. On 9 February 1985, two days before her tenth anniversary as leader of the Conservative Party, Prime Minister Margaret Thatcher gave a celebratory speech to national Young Conservatives. Security was the tightest yet seen at a British political event, with delegates queuing for more than an hour in the snow, crowding the pavement back to the Square. Handbag searches – though not for the lady, one presumes – were augmented by checks from a sniffing device for explosives.

'Ten more years,' they chanted. The Prime Minister was entering the 49th week of her epic struggle with Arthur Scargill and his striking coal miners. Mrs Thatcher accused them of Luddism. 'We have witnessed an ugly chapter in trade union history,' she declared.

Mrs Thatcher returned, to Bournemouth International Centre on 10 October 1986, but a painful sprained ankle caused her fighting speech to the Conservative Party Conference to be cut from 50 minutes to 35 minutes. The themes were 'popular capitalism' at home and Russian 'nuclear blackmail' overseas. Neil Kinnock was the opponent and the Prime Minister forecast that her party would stay in power until the next century. 'Jubilant Tories applauded for nine-and-a-half minutes,' Trevor Kavanagh of *The Sun* reported.

The Prime Minister was staying at the Highcliff Hotel which had thrown off its 'e' to avoid confusion with Highcliffe at Christchurch. It was only two years on from the Brighton bombing and there was a major security breach from which a twenty-nine year-old Poole taxi driver was lucky to escape alive. The 'kamikaze prankster' was in the sights of marksmen with high-velocity rifles three times that Friday. He began by screeching to a halt beside the Royal Bath Hotel, where many delegates were staying, and threw a package at the feet of policemen. Then he drove on along Exeter Road and repeated the process, with a briefcase, on the steps to the conference centre. Finally he sped uphill, along Priory Road and then into St Michael's Road, to the Highcliff Hotel. There the escapade ended in arrest as he crashed through two security barriers. The £1 million security operation had been embarrassingly compromised but there was no terrorist motive.

In 1987 there was more excitement as former Boscombe Football Club, now AFC Bournemouth, climbed into the second division of the Football League. Metal shuttering appeared on Boscombe shop fronts as the town braced itself for bouts of football hooliganism. It was a world away from the days of the St John's Lads as the club approached its centenary.

Empire diplomats and soldiers continued to retire to Bournemouth and Dorset as their predecessors had been doing for more than a century. Colonial premier Sir Roy Welensky (1907–91) came to Blandford in 1981, from white-ruled Southern Rhodesia, before

it became Zimbabwe on full independence. He had been a heavyweight boxer and railwayman in the Northern Rhodesian copper belt, organised trades union activities, and went into politics. He rounded off his career as Prime Minister of the short-lived Federation of Rhodesia and Nyasaland from 1956 to 1963. His last ten years were spent in Dorset. He died in Blandford Hospital and is buried in the Jewish Cemetery at Kinson.

Hal Geneen would have approved of the symbol of the new Bournemouth where Dennis C. Longwell, general manager of the Chase Manhattan Bank in Britain, planted a tree. It was in front of their new operations building, built by Costain Construction at Littledown, in 1986. Appropriately, the tree was a catalpa – the southern bean-tree – from the USA.

Dennis C. Longwell plants the catalpa to mark the arrival in Bournemouth of Chase Manhattan Bank in 1986.

JACKS of ALL TRADES

Operational Records
of TON Class Minesweepers and Minehunters

Editor: Peter Down, Honorary Secretary TCA

Research: Jeremy Stewart, TCA Historical Group

Pictures: Bob Dean, Rik Furnival and TCA Historical Archives

Printed by: Gipping Press Ltd, Needham Market, Suffolk

Jacks of All Trades
Operational Records of TON Class Minesweepers and Minehunters

ISBN 978 0 9570588 0 4

Published by TON Class Association
39 Anderson Close
Needham Market
Suffolk
IP6 8UB

www.tca2000.co.uk

First published in Great Britain in March 2012 by TCA
Second Edition November 2012

The TON Class Association has asserted its right
under the Copyright, Designs and Patents Act 1988
to be identified as the author of this work

All the photographs used in this book have been derived from TCA archives.
This repository has been derived from a number of sources, principally TCA members
and other sources in the public domain. Where it has not been possible to trace a
particular illustration to its original source, we request the owner to accept that
their photographs have been used in a good cause of which we hope they would approve.

Typeset in News Gothic

Printed and bound by
by Gipping Press, Needham Market, Suffolk

HMS SHAVINGTON
Fishery Protection Squadron
Lieutenant J. Lippiett RN Commanding Officer
1976-77

I am delighted to contribute a few words to "Jacks of All Trades", a summary of the operational records of each TON Class ship which served in the Royal Navy. The book is a companion volume to "Last of the Wooden Walls"; a matched pair of books produced by the TON Class Association to mark its 25th anniversary.

Jeremy Stewart and his team in the TCA Historical Group have done a magnificent job of research in compiling a wealth of detail about each of the ships in this most numerous class. I congratulate them on their great endeavours.

The TONs generate a strong sense of loyalty in all who served in them, despite the cramped conditions on board, the often uncomfortable ride in a seaway and not infrequent forays into danger during their deployments round the world.

I recall with pride and affection my own experiences of serving in TONs; initially in CURZON as a cadet in the Combined Cadet Force, subsequently in APPLETON in the Gulf as a Midshipman and, in the 1970's in command of SHAVINGTON in the Fishery Protection Squadron.

The mixture of hard work and play remains in the forefront of my memories of those happy days. A close-knit ship's company working in close harmony proved the strength of our successful operations, tinged with the ever-present sense of humour which was often the saving grace in challenging circumstances. As is always the case at sea, it is the men who form the true heart of our Service, and the crews of the TONs were second to none.

The TON Class Association does a marvellous job in keeping alive the comradeship of the ships and spirit of those times. I am very proud to be President of the Association and wish it, and all its members, the very best for the future. I hope that all who sailed in TONs will enjoy the book and look up references to their own times in their ships.

Rear Admiral John Lippiett CB, MBE
President of the TON Class Association
Chief Executive of the Mary Rose Trust

Jacks of All Trades
Operational Records of ships of the TON Class

This book has been produced as a companion to the book "Last of the Wooden Walls , a History of the TON Class " to mark the 25th Anniversary of the TON Class Association.

This volume provides a summary of the service of each of the ships of the TON Class that served in the Royal Navy between 1953 and 1993. Some ships had a long operational life, others quite short, having spent many years "arked" in reserve.

These records have been compiled primarily from Ship's Logs, Navigational Data Books and Commanding Officers' Reports of Proceedings. Any errors are attributable to the Editor, who would be pleased to learn of corrections to detail and to set matters aright via TON Talk.

HMS CONISTON First of the class to become operational April 1953.

Over the years 37 TONs were transferred to other navies and some continued to serve at sea for a considerable time. The last two in commission as warships were the Argentine ships Formosa and Chaco (formerly HM Ships Rennington and Ilmington), who were not de-commissioned until 2003 and broken up in 2005.

At least two other TONs are still at sea, although in much modified civilian form, as tour ships and diving vessels.

At the end of the Second World War it was generally accepted that the emphasis on mining had shifted from deeply laid moored mines to ground mines laid in the shallow approaches to ports and harbours. A design team was formed in Bath in 1947 and by 1949 had produced two designs of an advanced concept for inshore and coastal work. The types were to be further categorised as minesweepers and minehunters, but the hunter variant was put on hold due to lack of suitably sensitive sonar at that time.

The onset of the Korean War and discovery of new, highly sensitive, Russian magnetic mines accelerated production of the non-magnetic Coastal Minesweeper.

The result was a very sturdy and flexible craft, with a double mahogany hull over an aluminium frame, with non-magnetic fittings, capable of undertaking ocean passages, and able to sweep both moored and ground mines.

Their vital statistics were: Length 152 ft; Beam 28 ft; Draught 8 ft; Displacement 360 tons net, 425 tons gross; Designed Speed 15 knots on passage, 8 knots towing: Range 2300 nautical miles at 13 knots; Two diesel engines (originally Mirrlees V12 2500 hp, later Napier Deltics 3000 hp); Complement 3 Officers, 4 Chief/Petty Officers and 28 sailors, though this varied, depending upon deployment and operations and was often 5 Officers, 6 Chief/Petty Officers and 35 ratings.

Upperworks and many of the fittings were constructed from light aluminium alloy and other materials with the lowest possible magnetic field, to achieve optimum safety when sweeping for magnetic mines. The ships were protected from pressure mines by their low displacement and the threat from moored mines was greatly reduced by their shallow draught.

The ships were originally to have been named after insects, perhaps recalling the gunboats on the China Station in the 1920's, but in 1952 this proposal was dropped and the TONs were named after villages ending in "... ton" e.g. CONISTON, ASHTON, HOUGHTON, WILKIESTON, FISKERTON etc.

HMS WILTON 1973-94 The ultimate evolution of the TON design.
The world's first GRP [glass reinforced plastic] hull warship.

117 wooden-hulled TONs were built, the most numerous class of vessel ever to serve in the Royal Navy and the design was adopted by several other navies.

TONs saw action on the Suez canal (twice), Cyprus, in the Confrontation with Indonesia, the Persian and Arabian Gulfs and in Northern Ireland. In addition to minesweeping and mine hunting, they carried out roles as diverse as patrol craft for fishery protection duties and to counter piracy, illegal immigration, and terrorist gun-runners. They acted as gun platforms and diving tenders and were the mainstay of the Royal Naval Reserve.

Crew members, of all ranks, held responsibilities far beyond their years and many a future Admiral had his first experience of sea command in a TON minesweeper.

One famous Commanding Officer commented that ... "TONs had a well-deserved reputation for rolling, even on wet grass, but despite this and the privations of life in cramped conditions on board, the ships were very popular with all who served in them. Often unsung, certainly uncomfortable and sometimes in danger, the TONs went about their duties round the globe with the Royal Navy and in many other navies as well."

On 3rd December 1993 HMS NURTON, the last operational TON in RN service, was decommissioned at HM Naval Base Portsmouth after 37 years service.

There would be no more wooden fighting ships in the Royal Navy and thus came to an end the centuries-old tradition of the Wooden Walls of England.

**"Wooden Walls" painting by TCA member Tony Standish,
now exhibited in the Royal Maritime Club, Portsmouth**

HRH Prince Charles commanded HMS BRONINGTON in 1976-77.	**HMS SHERATON caught in the swell of the tail of a typhoon off Japan 1970**	**Minesweeper headquarters ship HMS WOODBRIDGE HAVEN and ships of the 104th Minesweeper Squadron exercise off Singapore 1959**

Laid Down:	2nd July 1951
Built by:	J I Thorneycroft, Southampton
Completed:	16th December 1953
Time to Build:	29 months
Commissioned:	5th January 1954 as Senior Officer 104th Minesweeping Squadron based Harwich
Years Fully Operational:	3 with RN

Outline of Operational Career:

9 Feb 54	Arrived Harwich as first Ton in new 104th MSS
Feb 54-May 56	Exercises and Visits in North European Waters
26 Aug-3 Sep 56	Passage to Malta
31 Oct 56	Sailed for Port Said for Operation MUSKETEER
24 Dec 56	Arrived Malta post MUSKETEER
14-17 Jan 57	First (and only) Cyprus Patrol
4-13 Feb 57	Passage to UK (Devonport)

Significant Events:

24-28 Nov 55	First Ton Class Squadron visit to London
6 Nov 56	Operation MUSKETEER. Wire Sweeping Group
	Second Ton to enter Port Said Outer Harbour.

Paid Off:	14th February 1957
Disposal:	Sold to RAN April 1961 and following refit at Blyth
	11th September 1961 Commissioned as HMAS SNIPE
	Passage to Australia Oct to Dec 1961.

Laid Down:	27 Nov 53
Built by:	Camper and Nicholson, Southampton
Completed:	18 Apr 56
Time to Build:	29 months
Commissioned:	24 Aug 56 for 108th Minesweeping Squadron based Malta
Years Fully Operational:	One year with RN.

Outline of Operational Career:

24 Aug-4 Sep 56	Passage to Malta, with PENSTON
20 Sep-14 Nov 56	First Cyprus Patrol (56 days)
15 Nov-21 Dec 56	At Port Said. Post-landing support role
Jan-Jun 57	Exercises and Visits in Central Mediterranean
17 Mar-24 Apr 57	Second Cyprus Patrol (39 days)
1 Jun 57	Exchanged Crews with DUFTON at Malta
7-18 Jun 57	Passage to UK. Paid off and Refit on arrival
1958-63	Reserve Fleet at Hythe, then Gibraltar

Significant Events:

28 Aug 56	Damage to M/S winch shaft during exercise
6-16 Sep 56	Alloy winch shaft replaced with mild steel.
15 Nov 56	Arrived at Port Said. Transferred to 104th MSS.
21-24 Dec 56.	Passage to Malta with WOODBRIDGE HAVEN
6 Mar 57	In night collision with PENSTON. Damaged.
May 57	Decision for ALDINGTON to return to UK
7-18 Jun	Passage to UK
Paid off:	19 Jun 57 at Chatham for Refit & Reserve.
Disposal:	Aug 1963. Sold to Ghana Navy as EJURA

HMS ALFRISTON

Laid Down:	17 Aug 51
Built by:	John I Thornycroft, Woolston
Completed:	16 Mar 54
Time to Build:	31 months
Commissioned:	1st May 1954 for 101st Minesweeping Squadron based Southampton, as WARSASH
Years Fully Operational:	29 – All with RNVR/RNR

Outline of Operational Career:

May 54-Jun 60	As HMS WARSASH, based Southampton
Jul 60-Dec 75	Renamed HMS KILMOREY, based Belfast
Jan 79-Jun 85	Reverted to ALFRISTON, based Southampton

Significant Events:

May-Jun 82	RNR Deployment to Gibraltar & Lisbon
May 84	RNR Deployment to Gibraltar & Lisbon
Paid Off:	June 1986
Disposal:	27 Nov 88 Sold to Brugse Scheepssloperij for Break Up

HMS ALVERTON   Pennant No. M1104

Laid Down:	25th June 1951
Built by:	Camper and Nicholson
Completed:	24th March 1954
Time to Build:	33 months
Commissioned:	8th June 1954 for 101st Minesweeping Squadron based London, as THAMES
Years Fully Operational:	7 (All with RNVR/RNR)

Outline of Operational Career:

1954-1961	Sea Training for London Division RNVR
	To reserve Hythe then towed to Singapore for Operational Reserve
1967	Towed back to Gibraltar for Reserve

Paid off:	December 1961
Disposal:	22 Feb 71 Commissioned as Irish Naval Ship BANBA

Laid Down:	9th July 1951
Built by:	Camper & Nicholson
Completed:	17th July 54
Time to Build:	34 months
Commissioned:	9th October 1954 for 101st Minesweeping Squadron based Liverpool as MERSEY
Years Fully Operational:	14 (All with RNVR/RNR)

Outline of Operational Career:

12 Sep 54	Arrived Liverpool for RNVR Training
Aug 56	Sea Training Deployment to Gibraltar
Nov 59	Name reverted to AMERTON
Dec 59-Mar 61	Deltic Engine Conversion in Devonport
25 Mar 61	Commissioned as HMS CLYDE, Glasgow
1961-70	RNR Training, Exercises and Visits in North European Waters
1 Oct 62	101st MSS renumbered as 10th MSS
9-25 Aug 63	To Gibraltar/Tangier for Ex ROCKHAUL 63
14-30 Aug 64	To Gibraltar/Lisbon for Ex ROCKHAUL 64
11-20 Aug 65	To Oporto for Ex ROCKHAUL III
13 Aug-11 Sep 66	To Gibraltar/Casablanca/Lisbon for Exercise ROCKHAUL IV
27 Aug-24 Sep 67	To Gibraltar for Ex ROCKHAUL V
08 Aug-5 Sep 69	To Gibraltar for Ex ROCKHAUL 69
23 Aug-19 Sep 70	To Gibraltar/Lisbon for Ex MAINHAUL
	Note: 2 Crews for above four exercises.

18 Oct 70	**Name reverted to AMERTON**
Paid Off:	18 Oct 70
Disposal:	20 Jul 71 Sold for breaking up at Bo'ness on Forth

Laid Down:	2nd April 1951
Built by:	Goole Shipbuilding Co. Ltd
Completed:	18th March 1954
Time to Build:	35 months
Commissioned:	23rd March 1954 for 104th Minesweeping Squadron based Harwich
Years Fully Operational:	12

Outline of Operational Career:

10 May 54	Joined 104th MSS at Harwich
18 Oct 54	Paid Off to Reserve. Crew to DARLASTON
Jan 55-May 56	Long Refit at Chatham
14 May 56	Commissioned as SO 105th MSS
25 Aug-2 Sep 56	Passage to Malta with 105th MSS
27 Oct-3 Nov 56	1st Cyprus Patrol (8 Days)
5 - 7 Nov 56	Operation MUSKETEER
9-16 Nov 56	2nd Cyprus Patrol (8 Days)
17-20 Nov 56	Passage to Malta
23 Nov-2 Dec 56	Passage to UK. Paid off to Reserve.
27 Mar 57	Commissioned for 100th MSS as SO
1 - 12 Sep 58	Passage to Malta to augment Inshore Flotilla for Cyprus Patrol
13 Sep–25 Nov 58	3rd Cyprus Patrol (66 days)
1-11 Dec 58	Passage to Portsmouth
10 Jun 59	9th MSS transferred base to Port Edgar
10 Aug 60	Paid off at Portsmouth for refit & reserve
25 Jun 62	Commissioned for 9th MSS as SO

20-31 Jul 62	Passage to Malta for Work-up
29 Aug-7 Sep 62	Passage to Aden for patrols
1-8 Jan 63	9th MSS transferred base to Bahrain
1963-65	Patrols, exercises and visits in Gulf Area
2-28 Oct 65	Passage Bahrain to Gibraltar
30 Oct 65	Paid off at Gibraltar for refit and reserve
7 Feb 67	Commissioned for operations off Aden
9-26 Feb 67	Passage to Aden for local patrols
19 May 67	Rejoined 9th MSS at Bahrain
2-18 Jun 67	Squadron patrols off Aden during 6 Day War
1968-Mar 1969	Patrols, exercises and visits in Gulf Area
23 Mar-7 Jun 69	Passage Bahrain to UK round South Africa

Significant Events:

Oct 54	Damaged in collision with dock wall at Harwich
5-6 Nov 56	Op. MUSKETEER. SO Influence Sweeping Group.
Jan 58	Fitted with partially enclosed bridge
Sep-Nov 67	Aden Patrol Ship during UK withdrawal. Last RN ship to leave Aden

Paid Off: 9 Jun 69

Disposal: 24 Sep 72 Sold for breaking up at Neath, S. Wales

HMS ASHTON

Laid Down:	14th October 1954
Built by:	Whites Shipyard Ltd, Southampton
Completed:	15th April 1958
Time to Build:	42 months
Commissioned:	3rd July 1958 for 108th Minesweeping Squadron (MSS) based Malta
Years Fully Operational:	13

Outline of Operational Career:

Aug 58	Passage to Malta
29 Aug-06 Sep 58	First Cyprus Patrol (9 days)
1 Jan-05 Feb 59	Second Cyprus Patrol (32 days)
29 May-30 Jun 59	Third Cyprus Patrol (30 Days)
1959-1969	Exercises and Visits in Mediterranean
1 Oct 62	108th MSS renumbered as 7th MSS
31 Mar 69	7th MSS left Malta for Gibraltar
04 Apr 69	Paid off to refit and reserve in Gibraltar
15 Apr 71	Commissioned for 2 weeks post refit trials
28 Aug 72	Commissioned for Fishery Protection Squadron

Significant Events:

3 Apr 64	Collision with SHAVINGTON while Team Sweeping
7 Dec 66	Recovery of survivors from MV HERAKLION
Jan 68	At Trapani to assist after Sicilian earthquake

Paid Off:	Late 1974
Disposal:	3 Aug 77 for breaking up at Blyth.

Laid Down:	18th March 1953
Built by:	Camper & Nicholson, Gosport
Completed:	5th July 1955
Time to Build:	28 months
Commissioned:	16th July 55 for 108th Minesweeping Squadron (MSS) based Malta
Years Fully Operational:	2 ½

Outline of Operational Career:

9-19 Sep 55	Passage to Malta with 108th MSS
26 Sep 55	Passage to Cyprus with 108th MSS
7 Oct-16 Nov 55	First Cyprus Patrol (31 days)
18 Dec 55-31 Jan 56	Second Cyprus Patrol (40 days)
4 Mar-7 Apr 56	Third Cyprus Patrol (31 days)
28 Aug-3 Oct 56	Fourth Cyprus Patrol (36 days)
19 Oct-3 Nov 56	Passage to UK
11 Nov 56	Paid off at Hythe, then Reserve Devonport
1957-64	Reserve at Devonport
29 May 64	Recommissioned for Local Service – Target towing & ARK ROYAL Planeguard
10 Jul 64	Joined VERNON Squadron (NURTON Crew)

Paid Off:	May 65
Disposal:	14 Apr 70 Sold to C H Rugg for breaking up at Bruges

Laid Down:	9 April 1951
Built by:	Goole Shipbuilding Co. Ltd
Completed:	30 July 1954
Time to Build:	39 months
Commissioned:	29 July 1956 for Vernon Training Squadron (VTS) based Portsmouth
Years Fully Operational:	27

Outline of Operational Career:

July 1956	Joined Vernon Training Squadron (VTS)
31 Jan 1959	Paid off for Deltic conversion
13 Oct 1960	Recommissioned for VTS
Jan 1965	Refit. Ships Co transferred to BADMINTON.
26 Jul 65	Recommissioned for service in Persian Gulf.
Sep 1965	Passage to Bahrain to join 9th MSS.
1965-71	Patrols, Exercises and visits in Gulf Area
14 Aug 71	Passage to Far East with YARNTON
17 Sep 71	Arrived Hong Kong .Conversion to Patrol Craft
Jun 72	Joined the 6th Hong Kong Patrol Craft Squadron
Jan 85	Relieved by HMS STARLING (PEACOCK Class)

Significant Events:

3 Mar 66	Grounded while on inshore patrol in Straits of Hormuz. Hull damage.
Sep 66	Bahrain to Gibraltar for Refit. Returned Bahrain Feb 67.
Jan 69	Bahrain to Singapore for refit. Returned Bahrain Jul 69.
28 Sep 75	During RAS with USN tanker, supplied with AVGAS, not Diesel
2 Aug 79	Typhoon 'Hope'. First Lieut. received CinC's Commendation for exceptional seamanship during 3 hour berthing.

Paid Off:	4th January 1985
Disposal:	Sold to Acorn Shipping of London on 10 May 1985 for breaking up at Hong Kong.

HMS BELTON Pennant No. M1199

Laid Down:	23rd August 1954
Built by:	J S Doig & Co, Grimsby
Completed:	31st May 1957
Time to Build:	33 months
Commissioned:	12th March 1958 for Fishery Protection Squadron (FPS) based Port Edgar
Years Fully Operational:	14

Outline of Operational Career:

13 Mar 58	Joined Fishery Protection Squadron at Port Edgar
1958-71	Fishery Patrols round UK coast, interspersed with minesweeping operations and exercises and visits to UK and Northern European Ports
1 Jan 68	Fishery Protection Squadron became 4th MCMS
23 Oct 71	Driven aground in a gale while at anchor in Loch Maddy on west coast of Scotland

Significant Events:

Oct 59	Involved in 18 day search for Crashed Victor Bomber in Irish Sea.
17 Oct 62	Present at Fleet Review by King Olav of Norway in the Forth
May 63	Took part in Operation CLEAR ROAD based on Esjberg (Live mines)
Jun 63	Visit to Karlstadt on Lake Vanern, Sweden (150 miles from open sea).
May 68	Took part in Operation NEW BROOM based on Borkum (Live Mines)
May 70	CO (Lt Cdr B E Seath) made Vice Admiral of the Manx Herring Fleet.
Mar 71	i/c Operation 'VARNE SWEEP' (VLCC Route Location) off Dover

Paid Off:	October 1971
Disposal:	Sold to Davies & Newman Ltd on 25 Nov 74 to be broken up at Gijon, North Spain

HMS BEVINGTON   Pennant No. M1108

Laid Down:	13th September 19 51
Built by:	Whites, Southampton (Itchen)
Completed:	9th March 1954
Time to Build:	30 months
Commissioned:	10th April 1954 for 104th Minesweeping Squadron (MSS) based Harwich
Years Fully Operational:	One with RN. Service with Argentina Navy unknown

Outline of Operational Career:

12 Apr 54	Joined 104th MSS at Harwich
1954-55	Exercises and Visits in N. European Waters - Frequent defects affected programme
July 1955	Paid Off to Refit, and Reserve at Hythe

Significant Events:

Dec 1954	104th Squadron Official Visit to London
Feb 1955	Minesweeping Demonstrations to NATO Staffs in Norway & Denmark

Paid Off:	July 1955
Disposal:	28th April 1967 Sold to Argentina as TIERRA DEL FUEGO

Laid Down:	21st September 1951
Built by:	Whites, Southampton (Itchen)
Completed:	25th May 1954
Time to Build:	32 months
Commissioned:	3rd October 1954 for 101st (RNR) Minesweeping Squadron (MSS), for Shoreham
Years Fully Operational:	32

Outline of Operational Career:

27 Jul 54	Allocated to Sussex RNR and arrived Shoreham
30 Oct 54	Renamed HMS CURZON
1954-60	Exercises, Visits and Training Periods
Oct 60	Reverted to BICKINGTON for Deltic Conversion
4 Mar 62	Transferred to Forth Division RNR based Leith
24 Mar 62	Renamed HMS KILLIECRANKIE
1962-75	Exercises, Visits and Training Periods
7 Jan 76	Transferred to Fishery Protection Squadron and reverted to BICKINGTON.
1976-86	UK Fishery Patrols, visits and exercises

Significant Events:

Oct 62	Visited by King Olav of Norway at LOCHINVAR
1963-69	Annual 4 wk Deployment with 10th MCMS to Gibraltar for Ex ROCKHAUL (Except Aug 65 - Attended Royal Fleet Review on Clyde)
May 68	Took part in live minesweeping Operation NEW BROOM, Borkum

Aug-Oct 70	Exercise MAINHAUL – 6 week deployment to Gibraltar/Italian Ports.
Dec 74	In collision with East German MV 'Sirrah' off Sheerness.
Jul 77	Rescued FV 'Artilleryman' kidnapped by French FV off Plymouth
Apr 82	CO & most of crew transferred to MV JUNELLA to deploy to Falklands as a minesweeper with 4 other converted FVs.
Sep 85	Arrested German FV 'Scombrus' in North Sea after 2 hour chase.

Paid Off: 31st July 1986

Disposal: 23rd August 1988 to Vickers Dismantling Ltd for break-up.

HMS BILDESTON

Laid Down:	18th May 1951
Built by:	D S Doig Ltd, Grimsby
Completed:	28th April 1953
Time to Build:	23 months
Commissioned:	28th April 1953 for Vernon Training Squadron (VTS) based Portsmouth
Conversion:	1966-68 to Minehunter, with Deltic Engines
Years Fully Operational:	24 - First Ton to be declared operational (August 1953)

Outline of Operational Career:

May 53	Joined Vernon Training Squadron.
1954	Refit Portsmouth correcting major defects found in the first operational Ton.
1954	Joined 50th MSS (Trials) based at Port Edgar.
1958-68	Reserve at Hythe, fully arked, then major refit
1 Nov 68	Commissioned for 1st MCM Squadron, remaining operational at Rosyth for the next 15 years
1968-86	Operations, exercises and visits
1 Jan 84	Transferred to new 3rd MCM Squadron at Rosyth

Significant Events:

Sep 53	Exercise 'MARINER' – the first NATO Exercise involving a Ton Class ship.
Sep 69	Visit to Gothenburg - Crew boarded MV 'Cooranga', adrift and a danger to shipping in hurricane force winds, and secured her safely.
28 Jun 77	Silver Jubilee Review at Spithead

Paid Off:	December 1986
Disposal:	Sold to Pounds Breakers, Portsmouth 20th July 1988, then sold on to Spanish Shipbreakers

HMS BLAXTON

Laid Down:	17th June 1954
Built by:	John I Thornycroft Ltd, Woolston, Southampton
Completed:	24th April 1956
Time to Build:	32 months
Commissioned:	23rd May 1956 for 105th Minesweeping Squadron (MSS) based Harwich
Years Fully Operational :	One year

Outline of Operational Career:

26 May 56	Joined 105th MSS at Harwich
25 Aug-2 Sep 56	Passage to Malta with 105th MSS
31 Oct-14 Nov 56	In Eastern Mediterranean
8 Dec 56–mid Jan 57	Cyprus Patrol
31 Jan-10 Feb 57	Passage to Portsmouth
11 Feb 57	Paid off to Deltic Conversion (unfinished)
1958-64	Reserve at Hythe
Apr 66	Towed to Singapore for Reserve
Apr 67	Towed back to Gibraltar for Reserve

Significant Events:

5-6 Nov 56	Took part in Operation MUSKETEER- Wire Sweeping Group during approach then Influence.

Paid Off:	11 Feb 57
Disposal:	Feb 71 Sold to Eire Navy at Gibraltar as LE FOLA

HMS BOSSINGTON

Pennant No. M1133

Laid Down:	1st September 1954
Built by:	John I Thornycroft, Southampton.
Completed:	11th December 1956
Time to Build:	27 months
Commissioned:	25th February 1958 for pitch stabilisation trials as part of Vernon Squadron
Conversion:	1964-65 to Minehunter
Years Fully Operational:	26

Outline of Operational Career:

27 Jan 59	Recommissioned for RNR Training and duties with ACR and DNR based at VERNON
Jan 59 -Jun 64	RNR training, exercises & visits in North European waters.
1 Oct 62	Vernon Squadron renamed 5th MSS
29 Jun 64	Paid off for Conversion to Minehunter
1 Oct 65	Recommissioned at Chatham for 11th MSS
19 Feb-12 Apr 66	Passage to Singapore
Apr-Jul 66	Carried out 4 periods Straits Patrol (32 days)
1 Oct 66	11th MCMS absorbed into 6th MCMS
1 Sep 69	6th MSS moved to Hong Kong as 6th PCS
1 Oct -13 Dec 71	Passage to UK round Africa with MAXTON and HUBBERSTON
1 Jan 72	Joined new 2nd MCMS based at Portsmouth
1972-1987	Minehunting, Exercises and Visits
May-Dec 73	Attached to new STANAVFORCHAN

Mar-Sep 74	Deployed to Mediterranean for Operation RHEOSTAT (Suez Canal Clearance)
1976, 1978 & 1984	Attached STANAVFORCHAN for 4-6 months
Jun-Nov 84	Deployed to Mediterranean, then Gulf of Suez -

Significant Events:

9 Oct 62	Collided with SHERATON at Portsmouth
	Sep-Oct 68 Visit to North Australia (Mackay, Cairns)
	15 Feb 70 6th PCS changed funnel badge from Blackfoot to red Chinese Dragon
30 Nov 71	Towed ZULU (Defective Main Engine) from River Gambia to Dakar, West Africa
1 Nov 78	Grounded Loch Tarbert. Towed to Portsmouth for 12 month refit

Paid off: 2nd March 87

Disposal: 25th January 1989 Sold to Brugse Scheepssloperij for break up

Laid Down:	1st June 1951
Built by:	Richards Ironworks Ltd., Lowestoft
Completed:	29th April 1954
Time to Build:	35 months
Commissioned:	29th April 1954 for 104th Minesweeping Squadron (MSS) based Harwich.
Years Fully Operational:	14 Years

Outline of Operational Career:

Feb 55	NATO Minesweeping demonstrations in Norway & Denmark
Aug 55	Transferred to 105th MSS based Harwich
Jun 56	Joined 50th MSS based Port Edgar
Nov 58-Feb 60	Paid off for conversion to Deltic Engines
Mar 60	Solent Division RNR as WARSASH

Significant Events:

Aug-Sep 63	Deployed to Gibraltar for ROCKHAUL 63
	Feb-Mar 65 Operation STOP GAP – Deployment to Madeira, C. Verde Islands and West Indies
Aug-Sep 66 & 67	Deployed to Gibraltar - ROCKHAUL 66 & 67
9 Aug 66	Assisted in rescue of crew of SS 'Polly' - Sank following collision off Gibraltar.
9 Sep 68	Collision with NORTHUMBRIA (QUAINTON)

Paid Off:	5th May 1969
Disposal:	25th November 1974 - Towed to Hayle for dismantling by Stanley Ferry Dismantlers Ltd.

Laid Down:	25 September 1951
Built by:	Richards Ironworks, Lowestoft
Completed:	9 July 1954
Time to Build:	34 Months
Transferred:	October 1954 to HMS CAMBRIA (South Wales Division RNVR) based Cardiff
Conversion to Minehunter:	6 July 1967 to 16 December 1968 at Portsmouth
Years Fully Operational:	33

Outline of Operational Career:

May 1955.	Renamed HMS ST DAVID
19 Oct 61	Reverted to BRERETON. Refit at Devonport
1962-64	Reserve at Hythe
18 Jan 65.	Commissioned for Fishery Protection Squadron.
Nov 66.	Paid off for Minehunter Conversion
16 Dec 1968.	Commissioned for 9th MCMS based at Bahrain
22 Apr- 04 Jul 69	Passage to Persian Gulf round Africa

1 Oct-10 Dec 71	Passage to UK round Africa.
Jan 72.	Fishery Protection Squadron based Port Edgar.
10 Jan-2 Nov 79	Long Refit at Gibraltar
21 Nov 79	Transferred to Tyne Division RNR based Newcastle
6 Apr 81.	Transferred to Mersey Division RNR
20 Jan 1986.	Transferred to 3rd MCMS based Rosyth
25 Jul 88- 1 Jun 89	On loan to Fishery Protection Squadron

Significant Events:

May 65	Arrested 7 FVs in 4 weeks - Total Fines £3,200
21 Oct 65	Salvage of MV 'Lady Serena' after fire onboard
25 Apr–13 May 74	With RECLAIM, salvaged ditched helicopter off Harstad, North Norway from 350ft. World record.
27 Feb 1976	Collision with FV 'Cyrano' off Hartlepool. 4 ft gash in hull below waterline.
Mar-Aug 76	Repairs
8 Jun 78	Major Engineroom Fire. Repairs took 2 months.

Paid Off: 30th April 1991

Disposal: 28th November 1992 to Scheepsslopjeri of Bruges for break up.

Laid Down:	30th May 1951
Built by:	Cook, Welton and Gemmell Ltd, Beverley
Completed:	4th March 1954
Time to Build:	34 Months
Commissioned:	9th March 1954 for 104th Minesweeping Squadron (MSS) based Harwich
Converted to Minehunter:	June 1966 to September 1968 at Devonport
Years Fully Operational:	30

Outline of Operational Career:

14 May 54	Joined 104th MSS at Harwich
29 Mar 55	Transferred to 105th MSS based at Harwich
Jul 56	Paid Off at Hythe. Refit and reserve.
17 Apr 63	Commissioned for service in Plymouth Command
May 66	Paid off for Conversion to Minehunter
Oct 68	Commissioned at Plymouth for 9th MSS
28 Jan-15 Apr 69	Passage to Bahrain round Africa.
2 Oct –10 Dec 71	Passage to UK round Africa

15 Dec 71	Joined Fishery Protection Squadron
18 Nov 79	Transferred to 1st MCMS based Rosyth.
1 Jan 84	Transferred to 3rd MCMS based Rosyth
26 Oct 87	Loaned to Fishery Protection Squadron
25 Sep 89	Reverted to 3rd MCMS
14 Apr 91	Transferred to Fishery Protection Squadron
21 Sep 93	Last Ton (with SHERATON) to leave Rosyth

Significant Events:

11-19 Dec 74	Wreck survey of HMS VANGUARD in Scapa Flow. (Sunk 9th July 1917 following internal explosion).
15 May 76	BRINTON displayed 'Banana' emblem on Bridge
16 Aug 13-Oct 84	Took part in Operation HARLING-Mine Clearance in Gulf of Suez based at Adibaya, Egypt.

Paid Off: 5th October 1993

Disposal: Sold to Pounds of Portsmouth January 1998

Laid Down:	30th May 1951
Built by:	Cook, Welton & Gemmell Ltd, Beverley, Yorkshire
Completed:	4th June 1954
Time to Build:	36 Months
Commissioned:	September 1954 for 101st (RNVR) Squadron as HMS HUMBER, based ` Hull
Years Fully Operational:	31
Conversion to Minehunter:	December 1963 to February 1965 at Rosyth

Outline of Operational Career:

Oct 1954	Named HMS HUMBER. Joined 101st MSS.
May 1958	Reverted to BRONINGTON
Sep 1958	Reserve Chatham then Deltic Conversion at Rosyth
Mar 1960	Recommissioned for 50th MSS (Trials) at Portland
Oct 1961	Transferred to 51st MSS (later 1st MHS) at Port Edgar
Dec 1963	Paid off for conversion to Minehunter at Rosyth
Dec 1965	Joined 1st MCM Squadron based Rosyth
Sep 1978	Transferred to 2nd MCMS as SO based Portsmouth.
Jul 1983	Attached to STANAVFORCHAN (to Dec 83)
Jun 1988	Paid off at Portsmouth

Significant Events:

Mar 1960	Collision in Forth. Damage to stem. Repairs 6 weeks.
Mar 1973	Rescued 8 men and a woman from Dutch Coaster Aground off Co. Down
Feb 1976	Lt HRH The Prince of Wales took command (to Dec 76)
Nov 1976	HM The Queen visited ship in Pool of London
Apr 1981	Assisted HMS ALACRITY in standing by FV 'Pentille' Taking water off Plymouth. Pumping out failed so BRONINGTON ordered to sink FV with Bofors.

Paid Off: 30th June 1988

Disposal: 25th January 1989. Transferred to Trafford Park Development Corporation for display as preserved warship Later transferred to Historic Warships, Birkenhead. Now neglected and closed to the public.

HMS BURNASTON Pennant No. M1116

Laid Down:	3rd May 1951
Built by:	Fleetlands, Gosport
Completed:	3rd March 1954
Time to Build:	34 Months
Commissioned:	March 1954 for 104th Minesweeping Squadron (MSS) based Harwich
Years Fully Operational:	8

Outline of Operational Career:

Apr 1954	Joined 104th MSS at Harwich
Nov 1954	Placed in Reserve at Chatham, following refit.
Mar 1957	Recommissioned for 100th MSS based Portsmouth
Sep 1958	Paid off for Deltic Conversion at Sheerness
Mar 1959	Commissioned for 108th MSS based Malta.
Mar 1962	Paid off at Malta. Towed to Gibraltar. Docking & Reserve
Sep 1965	Recommissioned for 9th MSS based Bahrein.
Feb 1967	Returned to Gibraltar for Refit Mar-Jun.
Jun 1967	Attached to 7th MSS based Malta. Cyprus Patrols
Aug 1967	Lent Fishery Protection Squadron based Port Edgar
Nov 1967	Passage from UK round Africa. Arrived Bahrain Mar 68
Feb 1968	Rejoined 9th MSS at Bahrain
Mar 1969	Passage to UK round Africa, Arrived Portsmouth Jun 69

Significant Events:

Jun 1967	Suez Canal closed by war while on passage to Bahrain
Oct 1959	MV 'Deniz' scuttled while being searched off Cyprus
Apr 1961	SHAVINGTON collided with BURNASTON during Passage manoeuvres. SHAVINGTON serious damage

Paid Off:	9th June 1969
Disposal:	29 Mar 71 Sold to Metrec, Newhaven for breaking up.

HMS BUTTINGTON

Laid Down:	26th November 1951
Built by:	Fleetlands Shipyard Ltd, Gosport
Completed:	4th June 1954
Time to Build:	30 months
Commissioned:	September 1954 for 101st (RNVR) Minesweeping Squadron based Bristol
Years Fully Operational:	13 (All with RNVR/RNR)

Outline of Operational Career:

20 Sep 54	Transferred to Severn Division RNVR
1 Jan 55	Renamed HMS VENTURER
11 Nov 60	Paid off for Deltic Conversion
Nov 61	Re-commissioned as HMS THAMES for London Division RNR, based Southampton
Nov 62-Jan 63	Temporary attachment to VERNON Training Squadron with MONKTON's crew.

Significant Events:

Jul 63	Took part in Operation CABLEWAY (joint RN/RNR live minesweeping) based on Den Helder, Holland
Jul 64	Near collision with CURZON (FITTLETON)

Paid Off:	6th April 1967
Disposal:	Sold to Metrec at Newhaven 12th May 1970 for break up.

Laid Down:	18th February 1952
Built by:	Wivenhoe Shipyard Ltd, Colchester
Completed:	12th November 1954
Time to Build:	32 months
Commissioned:	4th January 1955 for 105th Minesweeping Squadron (MSS), based Harwich
Years Fully Operational:	3

Outline of Operational Career:

13 Jan 55	Arrived Harwich as SO 105th MSS
28 Mar 56	Started Major Refit at Chatham – Sheathed
13 Dec 56	Recommissioned for service in 105th based Malta.
19 Dec 56	Paid off into Reserve (for 8 years)
Oct-Nov 58	Towed to Aden by Tug PROSPEROUS for Reserve
Oct 63	Towed to Malta by Tug TYPHOON for refit
Nov 64	Towed to Aden by Tug REWARD for Reserve
20 Jan 65	Commissioned at Aden for 9th MSS (Aden)
Jan 65-Jun 66	South Arabian Coast and Gulf of Aden Patrols
22 Jul-14 Aug 66	Passage to UK

Significant Events:

1955	No major defects in first year.
Dec 1956	6 days in commission. Force reductions post Op. MUSKETEER.
Jun 66	Involved in final withdrawal from Aden

Paid Off:	September 1966
Disposal:	Sold via C H Rugg 17th June 1968 for break up at Bakkerzonen, Bruges

HMS CARHAMPTON

Pennant No. M1119

Laid Down:	9th November 1953
Built by:	Wivenhoe Shipyard Ltd, Colchester
Completed:	30th May 1956
Time to Build:	31 months
Commissioned:	19th November 1956 for 104th Minesweeping Squadron (MSS), based Malta
Years Fully Operational:	2

Outline of Operational Career:

26 Nov 56	Deployed to Malta
17 Dec 56	Started first Cyprus Patrol
1957-58	8 periods of Cyprus Patrol, and MCM Exercises
9 Oct 58	Paid off to Reserve at Malta
Apr 59	Towed to Aden by Tug ENFORCER for Reserve
Nov 63	Towed to Malta by Tug TYPHOON for Refit
Nov 64	Towed to Aden by Tug SEA SALVOR for Reserve
20 Jan 65	Commissioned at Aden for 9th MSS (Aden)
26 Jan-26 Mar 65	South Arabian Coast and Gulf of Aden Patrols
27 Mar 65	Paid Off and reverted to Local Reserve - Aden
5-22 Nov 65	Passage to UK (Ferry Crew)

Significant Events:

25 Feb 58	Stood by SS 'AFRICAN MARQUIS' in Kaso Straits (East of Crete)

Paid Off:	27th March 1965
Disposal:	Sold to Kitson Vickers at Plymouth 22nd June 1970 for breaking up

Laid Down:	28th January 1952
Built by:	Montrose Shipyard Ltd
Completed:	2nd April 1954
Time to Build:	28 Months
Commissioned:	6th April 1954 for VERNON Training Squadron (VTS) based Portsmouth
Years Fully Operational:	11 (all in Minesweeping Training Squadrons)

Outline of Operational Career:

May 54	Joined VERNON Training Squadron at Portsmouth
1955 & 56	Annual refits due to frequency of defects
1959	Minesweeping equipment trials throughout year
1 Oct 1962	VERNON Squadron renamed 5th MSS
Jul 63-Feb 64	Extended Refit at Portsmouth

Significant Events:

1959	Helicopter Minesweeping Trials in Solent

Paid Off:	31 May 1965
Disposal:	24th April 1970 to Metal Recoveries (Newhaven) Ltd for break up

HMS CHAWTON

Laid Down:	29 November 1955
Built by:	Fleetlands Shipyard, Gosport
Completed:	23 July 1958
Time to Build:	32 Months
Commissioned:	9 October 1958 For 104th MSS, based in Malta
Years Fully Operational:	15

Outline of Operational Career:

30 Oct 58	Arrived Malta. Joined 104th MSS
1958-59	3 periods Cyprus Patrol
21 Oct 59	Deployed to Far East with WOODBRIDGE HAVEN
30 Nov 59	Arrived Singapore
1961-62	Exercises and visits. Anti-piracy patrols.
1963	North Borneo river patrols.
1964-65	Sarawak and Singapore Straits patrols
Sep 65	Paid off and recommissioned as SO 9th MSS
Oct 65	Passage to Bahrain
1966-67	Gulf and Straits of Oman Patrols. Exercises
May 67	Passage to Gibraltar for Refit
Dec 67	Passage to Bahrain round Africa
1968-69	9th MSS based Bahrain
Mar 69	Passage to Gibraltar for refit then Reserve.
Nov 71	Recommissioned to replace BELTON in FPS.

Significant Events:

8-22 Dec 62	Supported Limbang Raid. Two seamen wounded.
9 Mar 72	Boarded French FV 'Shetland' in Channel following Hot Pursuit
10 Oct 74	Boarded 2000 ton Bulgarian Trawler 'Aurelia' while night fishing

Paid Off:	28 February 1975
Disposal:	24 Jun 1977 at Tees Marine service, Middlesborough

HMS CHEDISTON   Pennant No. M1121

Laid Down:	30th April 1952
Built by:	Montrose Shipyard Ltd
Completed:	28th September 1954
Time to Build:	29 months
Commissioned:	10th December 1954 for 101st Minesweeping Squadron based Dundee
Years Fully Operational:	2

Outline of Operational Career:

14th December 54	Arrived Dundee for Tay Division RNR
1955-57	RNVR Training, Exercises and Visits in North European Waters
11 Aug 55	Renamed HMS MONTROSE
Sep 1957	Name reverted to CHEDISTON on relief by HMS NURTON

Paid Off:	September 1957
Disposal:	21st April 1961
	Purchased by RAN. Commissioned as HMAS CURLEW on 21st August 1962
	Pictured above as HMAS CURLEW

HMS CHILCOMPTON

Laid Down:	1st September 1951
Built By:	Herd & MacKenzie Ltd, Buckie
Completed:	8th October 1954
Time to Build:	37 months
Commissioned:	13th June 1962 at Portsmouth for 9th MSS based Aden
Years Fully Operational:	7

Outline of Operational Career:

21 Oct 54	Joined Reserve Fleet at Hythe following preservation
1962	Refit at Camper & Nicholson to prepare for service.
20 Jul 62	Deployed to Malta for Work-up
7 Sep 62	Arrived Aden. Local and Southern Gulf Patrols.
8 Jan 63	9th MSS arrived at new base in Bahrain,
1963	Patrolling Aden area and Southern Gulf.
1964-65	Gulf Patrols and Exercises, some with Iranian Navy
14 Oct 65	Left Bahrain to reduce to Reserve in Gibraltar
Apr 67	Commissioned for Service in Fishery Protection Squadron.
22 Jun 67	Arrived Port Edgar, then 3 month docking due serious defect
Sep 67-69	Fishery Protection Patrols

Significant Events:

4 Dec 62	Assisted MV CAPTANTIONIS aground on Perim Island
Oct 68	Towed HMS KINGSFORD from Aberdeen to Port Edgar

Paid Off:	18th April 1969
Disposal:	November 1971 to Pounds Ship Breakers, Havant, Hants for scrapping.

Laid Down:	12th March 1952
Built By:	Richards Ironworks, Lowestoft
Completed:	18th February 1954
Time to build:	23 months
Commissioned:	March 1955
Years fully Operational:	14

Outline of Operational Career:

31 Mar 55	Joined 104th MSS at Harwich
1955-56	Exercises and Visits in North European Waters
28 Aug 56	Deployed to Malta with 104th and 105th MSS
23 Oct 56	Sailed for UK escorting Inshore squadrons
Dec 56	Paid off to Reserve Fleet, Hythe (to 1962)
Feb 1962	Re-commissioned as SO of 50th MSS based Portland.
Oct 1962	Transferred to 5th MSS (Vernon Squadron)
4 Mar 63	Paid off to Reserve
1964-65	Attached to 5th MSS but operating independently
23 Oct 65	Paid off to reserve
8 Aug 66	Recommissioned as Plymouth Command CMS
1966-69	Independent operations in Plymouth Command.

Significant Events:

24 Nov 55	104th MSS Official Visit to London
26 May 67	R/V with 'Gipsy Moth'. Escort to Plymouth
Apr-May 68	Operation 'Tuskar' Search for Aer Lingus Viscount in Irish Sea (based Rosslare)
Paid Off:	1 January 1969
Disposal :	1 July 1970 – Sold to HK Vickers & Sons (Eng) for breaking up at Plymouth

HMS CONISTON

Laid Down:	14th June 1950
Built By:	John I Thorneycroft Ltd
Completed:	17th March 1953
Time to Build:	33 months
Commissioned:	18th March 1953

Outline of Operational Career:

1953-54	First of Class Sea Trials based HMS VERNON
13 Jul 54	Arrived Harwich to join 104th MSS
1954-56	Exercises and Visits in North European Waters
25 Aug 56	Sailed with 104th MSS for Malta and Work up
6 Nov 56	Took part in Operation MUSKETEER
21 Dec 56	Returned to Portsmouth
1 May 57	Joined new 100th MSS, based HMS VERNON
1957-58	Exercises and visits in North European waters
1 Sep 58	Deployed to Malta for Cyprus Patrols
12 Dec 58	Returned to Portsmouth for 100th MSS
1 Jun 59	100th MSS transferred to Port Edgar
1960-61	Refit at Chatham. To reserve Hythe, then Gibraltar

Significant Events:

6 Nov 1956	Operation MUSKETEER. Stand-by Danlayer

Paid Off:	March 1960
Disposal :	28 Jan 70 Sold to Metrec of Newhaven for break up.

HMS CRICHTON

Pennant No. M1124

Laid Down:	21st April 1952
Built By:	Doig's Grimsby Yard
Completed:	23rd April 1954
Time to Build:	24 months
Commissioned:	18th June 1954 for 101st RNVR Squadron, based Greenock

Outline of Operational Career:

18 Jun 54	Arrived Greenock as Sea Tender for Clyde Division
1954-60	RNR Exercises, Continuous & Weekend Training Periods
1961-62	Deltic Conversion and Major Refit at Rosyth
6 May 62	Recommissioned as HMS St DAVID for SW Division RNR
1 Oct 82	101st MSS renamed 10th MSS
1962-75	Exercises and Training Periods, mainly in Irish Sea
Apr 76	Recommissioned as HMS CRICHTON for Mersey RNR
1977-78	Long Refit for FPS service. Fitted Enclosed Bridge
Apr 78-1985	Recommissioned. Fishery Protection Squadron Patrols

Significant Events:

10 Aug 56	Escort to HMY BRITANNIA - West Coast of Scotland Tour
Aug-Sep 63	Deployment to Gibraltar with 10th MSS (ROCKHAUL 1)
Aug-Sep 64	Deployment to Gibraltar with 10th MSS (ROCKHAUL 2)
Feb-Apr 65	RNR Group Deployment to West Indies as Guardship
Aug 65	Deployment to Oporto with 10th MSS (ROCKHAUL 3)
Aug-Sep 66	Deployment to Gibraltar/Casablanca (ROCKHAUL 4)

Aug-Sep 67	Deployment to Gibraltar with 10th MSS (ROCKHAUL 5)
Aug-Sep 69	Squadron Deployment to Gibraltar (ROCKHAUL '69)
Aug-Sep 70	Squadron Deployment to Gibraltar (MAINHAUL '70)
Aug-Sep 71	Squadron Deployment to Gibraltar (MAINHAUL '71)
22 Oct 75	Hauled down Welsh Flag after 22 years service with RNR
1981 & 82	3 successful prosecutions of fishing vessels in each year
Dec 84	'Golliwog' emblem on bridge upset Manchester politicians

Paid Off: 4th October 1985

Disposal :   25th March 1987 To SB Queenborough for break up at Cairn Ryan

HMS CROFTON

Laid Down:	3 September 1956
Built by:	J I Thornycroft Ltd, Woolston, Southampton
Completed:	22nd August 1958
Time to Build:	23 months
Commissioned:	27th August 1958 for 108th MSS based at Malta
Years Fully Operational:	26

Outline of Operational Career:

3-14 Nov 58	Passage to Malta. Joined 108th MSS
Nov 58-Jan 59	First Cyprus Patrol
1959	4 Periods of Cyprus Patrol
1960-1961	Exercises and Visits in Mediterranean
Jul-Aug 61	Kuwait Emergency. 108th MSS to Bahrain & back
1 Oct 62	108th MSS became 7th MSS
1962-1968	Exercise and Visits in Mediterranean
31 Mar 69	7th MSS left Malta for Gibraltar for last time
Apr 1969	Paid off at Gibraltar and transferred to RNR (10th MSS)
5 May 69	Commissioned as HMS SOLENT based Southampton
1 Jan 76	Reverted to HMS CROFTON. Channel Group RNR
1978	Reallocated to North West Group based EAGLET
1981	Reallocated to North East Group based CALLIOPE

Significant Events:

Jun-Jul 67	Six Day War. Completed two periods Cyprus Patrol
Jan 68	Trapani (Sicily) Earthquake Relief
14 Apr 69	CROFTON's first return to UK for 11 years
24 Jun 78	Present at Silver Jubilee Review at Spithead
Paid Off:	1984
Disposal :	25th March 1987. Sold to Shipbreaking, Queensborough, Cairnryan for break up

HMS CUXTON

Laid Down:	23rd July 1952
Built By:	Camper & Nicholson, Southampton
Completed:	13th October 1954
Time to Build:	27 months
Commissioned:	October 1975 for Fishery Protection Squadron based Rosyth
Years Fully Operational:	15

Outline of Operational Career:

1954-61	At Hythe in Reserve
May 62-1975	At Gibraltar in Reserve (last Ton in reserve)
Oct 75	Commissioned for service in FPS
Feb 82	Transferred to 10th MCMS for Tay Division RNR
May 84	10th MCMS Training deployment to Gibraltar
1985	Transferred to Northern Ireland Squadron, based Faslane
Apr 88	Sustained severe hull damage. 5 month repairs Rosyth.

Significant Events:

24 Jun 77	Took part in Spithead Review

Paid Off:	1991
Disposal :	16 April 1992. Sold for breaking up at Bruges

Laid Down:	26 March 1952
Built By:	Whites Shipyard (Southampton) Ltd
Completed:	19 October 1954
Time to Build:	33 months
Commissioned:	19th January 1955 for 51st Minesweeping Squadron as SO, based Port Edgar
Years Fully Operational:	16

Outline of Operational Career:

1955	Trials, exercises and visits in Home Waters
Aug-Sep 56	Deployed to Malta with 51st and 232nd MSS
23 Oct 56	Sailed for UK with 51st and 232nd MSS (No longer required for Operation MUSKETEER)
30 Apr 57	Complete crew transfer from HMS BILDESTON
1958	Trials And Exercises in UK Waters
16 Mar 59	Paid off to Reserve and Refit. Tailshaft problems
1960	Converted to Deltic Engines in Rosyth
Mar 61	Transferred to 101st (RNR) MSS as HMS MONTROSE based at Dundee
1 Oct 62	101st MSS became 10th MSS
Aug 63/64/65	Deployed to Gibraltar for Exercise ROCKHAUL series
Aug 67	Deployed to Gibraltar for ROCKHAUL
Aug 69/70/71	Deployed to Gibraltar for ROCKHAUL & MAINHAUL

Significant Events:

May 68	Took part in Operation NEW BROOM (Live Minesweeping) based Den Helder
Paid Off:	June 1972
Disposal :	Bought by Willmetts of Southampton Nov 72 and passed to Pounds (Portsmouth) for breaking up in April 73

Laid Down:	30th September 1952
Built By:	Cook, Welton & Gemmell Ltd, Beverley
Completed:	5th October 1954
Time to Build:	24 months
Commissioned:	12th October 1954 for 104th MSS with HMS APPLETON's Crew
Years Fully Operational (RN):	3

Outline of Operational Career:

Oct 1954	Joined 104th MSS at Harwich
1955-56	Exercises and visits in Northern European waters
Aug-Sep 56	Deployed to Malta with 104th & 105th MSS
Jan 1957	Returned to UK. Based Harwich
Nov 1957	Paid off for Deltic Conversion and to Reserve
Feb 1960	Deployed to Far East with Ferry Crew
May 1960	Arrived Singapore

Significant Events:

Dec 1954	Inshore Flotilla Official Visit to London
5-6 Nov 56	Took part in Operation MUSKETEER - Danlayer
29 Feb 60	Diverted to Agadir for Operation SAMARITAN Earthquake Relief
24 May 60	Transferred to Royal Malayan Navy as KD MAHAMIRU at Singapore

Paid Off:	1960
Disposal :	Expended as a target in 1980

HMS DARTINGTON   Pennant No. M1203

Laid Down:	10th March 1955
Built By:	Philip & Sons, Dartmouth
Completed:	26th June 1958
Time to Build:	39 months
Commissioned:	4th September 1958 for 108th Minesweeping Squadron based in Malta
Years Fully Operational:	10

Outline of Operational Career:

26 Sep 1958	Joined 108th MSS at Malta
Oct-Nov 58	Joined Ton Group in Red Sea – Visit to Aqaba
Oct 1959	Transferred to 104th MSS
Oct-Nov 59	Passage to Singapore with 104th MSS
1960	104th MSS to Hong Kong for visit/exercises
1961-62	Exercises and Visits in China Sea area
1963	3 North Borneo Patrols, visits & Exercises
1964	7 North Borneo & 4 Singapore Straits Patrols
1965	4 North Borneo and 7 Singapore Straits Patrols
1966	4 North Borneo Patrols. Exercises & Visits
1967-69	Exercises and Visits in China Sea area

Significant Events:

Apr 61	Live Minesweeping Operation north of Sabah
25 Apr 61	Ran aground in Pitan Bay. Refloated
Dec 62	First North Borneo Patrol. Guardship Brunei Town
6 Sep 65	Sampan Incident in Singapore Straits
3 Jan 66	Fired on by Indonesians in Singapore Straits

Paid Off:	21st April 1969
Disposal :	12th February 1970 Sold to Wing Luen Hardwares Ltd of Hong Kong.

HMS DERRITON

Pennant No. M1128

Laid Down:	17th December 1952
Built by:	J I Thornycroft, Southampton
Completed:	1st June 1954
Time to Build:	19 months
Commissioned:	6th November 1954 for 101st (RNVR) MSS as HMS KILLIECRANKIE based Leith
Years Fully Operational:	7
Outline of Operational Career:	
1954-1961	Sea Training for Forth Division RNR, Exercises and Visits in N. European waters
Significant Events:	
26 Jun 55	Escorted HMY BRITANNIA out of Forth at start of HM THE QUEEN's State Visit to Norway
Paid Off:	16th October 1961 Thereafter, spent 1963-1970 in reserve at Hythe. Fittings made available for removal and transfer to HMS WILTON (first GRP Minehunter) from August 1970
Disposal:	23rd February 1971. Sold to A E Pierce & Sons, Canvey Island for breaking up at Pitsea

HMS DILSTON

Pennant No. M1168

Laid Down:	27th February 1954
Built By:	Cook, Welton & Gemmell, North Yorkshire
Completed:	20th July 1955
Time to Build:	17 Months
Commissioned:	10th October 1955 for 108th Minesweeping Squadron based at Malta
Years fully Operational:	2

Outline of Operational Career:

11 Oct 55	Sailed for Malta, via Brest. (Arrived 27 Oct)
Nov-Dec 55	First Cyprus Patrol
Mar-Apr 56	Second Cyprus Patrol, inc visit to Beirut
Jun-Jul 56	Third Cyprus Patrol
18 Nov 56	Sailed for Port Said with FLORISTON
Nov-Dec 56	Fourth Cyprus Patrol
Jan-Mar 57	Fifth Cyprus Patrol
May-Jun 57	Sixth Cyprus Patrol
(Jul-Aug 57)	(Seventh Cyprus Patrol)
Oct 57	Returned to UK. Crew transferred to STUBBINGTON
1958-1963	Reserve Fleet at Hythe

Significant Events:

21-24 Nov 56	At Port Said as relief CMS post Op. MUSKETEER
26 Nov 56	Lieutenant J M H Cox took command. Later Vice Admiral Sir John Cox, first President of TON Class Association
April 1964	Transferred to Malaysian Navy as KD JERAI

Paid Off:

Disposal:	1984 by Malaysia

Laid Down:	3rd July 1953
Built By:	Goole Shipbuilders, Goole
Completed:	29th July 1955
Time to Build:	25 months
Commissioned:	September 1955 for 108th Minesweeping Squadron based at Malta
Years Fully Operational:	8

Outline of Operational Career:

9-20 Sep 55	Passage to Malta with Inshore Flotilla
Sep-Nov 55	First Cyprus Patrol, inc visit to Beirut
1956	Completed 4 periods of Cyprus Patrol
Nov 1956	Operation MUSKETEER
1957-58	Completed 8 Periods of Cyprus Patrol
May 1959	Paid off to Reserve in Malta
Mar-May 60	Towed by tug AGILE to Singapore
Jun 60-May 62	Reserve Fleet Singapore
16 May 62	Recommissioned for 120th MSS based Hong Kong
1 Oct 62	120th MSS became 8th MSS. Exercises/Visits
1964-66	Completed 10 periods North Borneo Patrol
Jan-Apr 67	Returned to UK via Suez Canal
May 67-Apr 69	RNR service as HMS THAMES based Southampton

Significant Events:

28 Aug 56	Ran aground off C. Arnauti, NW Cyprus. Refloated.
6 Nov 56	Influence Sweeper into Port Said
17 Nov 56	One of 3 Tons to sweep Suez Canal (to 30 km mark)
3 Apr 59	Completed 13th Cyprus Patrol (Most by any Ton).

Paid Off:	12th April 1969
Disposal:	June 1977. For break up at Ligura Marine, Sittingbourne

HMS EDDERTON   Pennant No. M1111

Laid Down:	18th May 1951
Built By:	J.S. Doig & Co, Grimsby
Completed:	10th March 1954
Time to Build:	34 months
Commissioned:	16th March 1954 as SO of 104th Minesweeping Squadron based Harwich
Years Fully Operational:	3 (as CMS)
Conversion:	1964-65 To Coastal Survey Vessel

Outline of Operational Career:

1954-55	Exercises and Visits in North European Waters
24 Apr 56	Transferred to new 105th MSS as SO
Aug-Sep 56	Escorted Inshore Minesweeper Squadrons to Malta
6 Nov 56	Took part in Operation MUSKETEER
1957	Completed one Cyprus Patrol, then returned to UK and paid off for Deltic Conversion and Reserve.
1957-64	In Reserve at Hythe
1964-65	Conversion to Coastal Survey Vessel
20 Jul 64	Recommissioned as HMS MYRMIDON
1965-1968	East Coast and Channel Surveys

Significant Events:

Dec 54	Squadron Visit to Pool of London
Feb 55	Ton Class Minesweeping Demonstration to NATO Officers in Norway and Denmark
6 Nov 56	Influence sweeping approaches to Port Said

Paid Off (as CMS):	1957
Disposal:	14th March 1969 Sold to Malaysian Navy & re-named PERANTAU Details of final disposal by Malaysia unknown

Laid Down:	26th March 1953
Built By:	Camper & Nicholson, Southampton
Completed:	18th May 1955
Time to Build:	26 months
Commissioned:	June 1955 for 108th Minesweeping Squadron based Malta
Years Fully Operational:	2 ½

Outline of Operational Career:

09 Sep 55	Sailed from UK with 108th MSS
20 Sep 55	Arrived Malta
1955-56	Two Periods of Cyprus Patrol
08-15 Nov 56	At Port Said
21 Nov 56	Recommissioned at Malta as SO of 108th MSS
21 Dec 56	Last Ton to leave Port Said post Op. MUSKETEER
Jan 57	Transferred to 104th MSS as Senior Officer (SO)
1957	Cyprus Patrols and Exercises
Jan 58	Returned to UK. Crew transferred to WALKERTON as SO of 104th MSS
1959-1962	Reserve Fleet, Gibraltar

Paid Off:	January 1958
Disposal :	3rd April 1964 Transferred to Malaysian Navy as KD KINABALU Details of final disposal in Malaysia unknown

Laid Down:	14th March 1953
Built By:	Camper & Nicholson, Southampton
Completed:	16th August 1955
Time to Build:	29 months
Commissioned:	26th August 1955 for 108th Minesweeping Squadron based Malta
Years of Operational Service::	3 (in RN)

Outline of Operational Career:

11 Oct 55	Sailed from UK
04 Nov 55	Arrived Malta, via Brest & Bizerta
1956	Completed 4 Cyprus Patrols: in 'Running Reserve'
1957	Completed 4 Cyprus Patrols
1958	Completed 3 Cyprus Patrols
27 Oct 58	Paid off to Reserve (Malta)
23 Nov 58	Crew flew to UK to commission WOOLASTON
08 Oct 59	Towed to Aden as Theatre Reserve
Nov 64	Sailed to UK with scratch crew (via Palermo)
1965	Started Refit at Devonport, subsequently terminated

Significant Events:

05-06 Nov 56	Operation MUSKETEER as Influence Sweeper.

Paid Off:	27th October 1958
Disposal:	17th June 1968. For break up by Metal Recoveries (Newhaven) Ltd

Laid Down:	1955
Built by:	J S Doig, Grimsby
Completed:	18th April 1957
Time to Build:	26 months
Commissioned:	15th June 1957 for 104th Minesweeping Squadron at Malta
Years Fully Operational:	11

Outline of Operational Career:

30 Jun 57	Sailed UK for Malta. Completed one Cyprus Patrol
1958	Completed 3 Cyprus Patrols
21 Oct 59	Sailed for Singapore with WOODBRIDGE HAVEN
30 Nov 59	Arrived Singapore
1960-62	North Borneo Patrols, Hong Kong and exercises
1963-64	North Borneo Patrols supporting Army
1965	Singapore Straits and Borneo Patrols
1966	Singapore Straits Patrols (to March)
Jan-Oct 67	Attached to 8th MCMS based Hong Kong
Jan-Apr 68	Passage to UK via South Africa

Significant Events:

1959	Searched Bulgarian Freighter off Cyprus military stores
3 Jan 60	Picked up survivors with PUNCHESTON from sinking Liberty Ship VALLEY FORGE in Indonesian waters.
26 Apr 61	Attempted to tow DARTINGTON, aground in Paitan Bay, N. Borneo. Hull damaged aft while passing tow to WOODBRIDGE HAVEN
4-5 May 61	Boarded 2 Kumpits with pirates onboard

11-22 Dec 62	Supported action at Limbang by 42 Cdo RM from Brunei Lt Cdr J.J. Black (CO 61-63) awarded MBE
04 Jan 64	Major Fire in Engine Room while on Borneo Patrol
14 Jun 64	Intercepted sampan with 10 saboteurs. Killed 3
Aug 65	Lt Cdr C D Prentis (CO 64-66) awarded DSC
Paid Off:	April 1968
Disposal:	1971 Sold to Pounds. Broken up by Henderson Merez, Dartford

HMS FITTLETON

Laid Down:	15th September 1952
Built By:	White's Shipyard, Itchen, Southampton
Completed:	28th January 1955
Time to Build:	28 months
Commissioned:	16th November 1960 for 101st (RNVR) Squadron as HMS CURZON based Shoreham
Years fully operational:	15

Outline of Operational Career:

1955-1960	In Reserve at Hythe (Arked)
1960-62	Sussex Division RNR Sea Tender (HMS CURZON)
1 Oct 62	101st MSS renamed 10th MSS
10-24 Aug 63	Deployed to Gibraltar for Exercise ROCKHAUL
Aug-Sep 64	To Gibraltar for Exercise ROCKHAUL 2
Aug-Sep 65	To Gibraltar for Exercise ROCKHAUL 3
Aug 66	To Gibraltar for Exercise ROCKHAUL 4
Aug-Sep 67	To Gibraltar for Exercise ROCKHAUL 5
1-10 May 68	Took part in Operation NEW BROOM (live sweeping)
Aug-Sep 69	To Gibraltar for Exercise ROCKHAUL 69
Aug-Sep 70	To Gibraltar For Ex. MAINHAUL and Visit to La Spezia
Aug-Sep 71	To Gibraltar for Exercise MAINHAUL 71
Sep 72	Took part in Major NATO Exercise 'STRONG EXPRESS'
Aug-Sep 73	Deployed to Canada for Exercise MAPLEHAUL 73
Sep 74	Took part in NATO Exercise 'NORTHERN MERGER'
31 Dec 75	Name reverted to HMS FITTLETON-Channel Group RNR

Significant Events:

20 Sep 76	Sunk after collision in Channel with HMS MERMAID during RAS, with loss of 12 members of her crew. Largest peacetime loss in recent RN history
Paid Off:	September 1976
Disposal:	20th September 1977. Sold to Liguria Maritime, Sittingbourne for scrap.

Laid Down:	19th March 1953
Built by:	White's Shipyard, Southampton
Completed:	7th October 1955
Time to Build:	31 months
Commissioned:	14th June 1962 for 9th Minesweeping Squadron(MSS) based at Aden
Years Fully Operational:	3

Outline of Operational Career:

1955-1960	In Reserve at Hythe
1961-62	Refitting for service in Middle East
20 Jul 62	Sailed for Aden with 9th MSS
1 Jan 63	9th MSS base move to Bahrein
1963-65	Exercises, Visits and Patrols in Gulf and Arabian Sea
17 Sep 65	Sailed for Gibraltar on relief by HMS BEACHAMPTON
9 Oct 65	Arrived Gibraltar. Paid off to reserve.

Significant Events:

3 to 6 Dec 62	Assisted MV 'Captantionis' aground off Perim Island

Paid Off:	20 Oct 65
Disposal :	28 Jul 69. Sold to Shipbreaking Queenborough, Kent for breaking up

HMS FLORISTON

Laid Down:	8th December 1952
Built by:	Richards Ironworks Ltd, Lowestoft
Completed:	19th August 1955
Time to build:	32 months
Commissioned:	2nd October 1955 for 108th Minesweeping Squadron based Malta
Years Fully Operational:	3

Outline of Operational Career:

11 Oct 55	Sailed for Malta with 3 other Tons
1955-56	4 Cyprus Patrols, exercises and visits.
Jun-Sep 56	Living Ship in Reserve in Sliema Creek, Malta CO & part Ship's Co to UK to commission SHAVINGTON
1957	3 Cyprus patrols. Exercises and visits
1958	3 Cyprus Patrols. Exercises and Visits
Sep 58	Paid off to reserve at Malta
Nov 59	Towed to Gibraltar
12 Dec 59	Recommissioned for Portland Trials Squadron to replace GLASSERTON
Jan-Mar 60	Portland Trials Squadron

Significant Events:

21-29 Nov 56	At Port Said to relieve Tons ex Op MUSKETEER
13-18 May 57	Towed from Cyprus to Malta by DILSTON.

Paid Off:	Apr 1960
Disposal:	27 Apr 68-Sold to Pounds of Portsmouth for use as a floating crane

Laid Down:	29th September 1952
Built by:	J S Doig (Grimsby) Ltd
Completed:	14th July 1954
Time to build:	22 months
Commissioned:	11th May 1956 as Senior Officer VERNON Training Squadron (VTS) based Portsmouth:
Years Fully Operational:	26 Years
Conversion to Minehunter:	September 1966 to October 1968 at Chatham

Outline of Operational Career:

May 56	Joined VERNON Squadron as SO
1956-1962	VERNON Squadron-Training, Exercises & Visits
May-Jul 62	Temporary service with London Div RNR
Aug 62-Aug 66	Operational Reserve at Hythe (Arked)
11 Oct 68	Commissioned for 9th MSS based Bahrain
May 69-Oct 71	Patrols and Exercises with 9th MSS based Bahrain
Oct-Dec 71	Returned to UK round South Africa
Dec 71	Joined 1st MCMS based Port Edgar
1971-1983	1st MCMS. Route Surveys, Exercises and Visits
1 Jan 84	Transferred to newly formed 3rd MCMS
30 Jun 86	Paid off to Stand-By Squadron
28 Oct 86	Recommissioned as Trials Ship

Significant Events:

10 Oct 57	Towed by Whirlwind Helo at 5 knots.
31 May 70	Operation OCCIDENTAL off Abu Musa
07 Jul 1970	Attempt to put out fire in MV 'Diffuri-Maadi' at entrance to the Gulf, with PUNCHESTON

Paid Off:	12 Dec 86
Disposal:	14 Oct 91 Broken up by Brugse Scheepssloperji, Belgium

Laid Down: 17th March 1953

Built by: J S Doig (Grimsby) Ltd

Completed: 31st December 1954

Time to build: 22 months

Commissioned:	23rd February 1955 for 50th Minesweeping (Trials) Squadron (MSS) based Port Edgar
Years Fully Operational:	26 years

Outline of Operational Career:

16 Mar 55	Joined 50th MSS at Port Edgar
1955-59	Minesweeping Trials. Frequent Dockings in Rosyth
15 Jun 59	50th MSS transferred to Portland as 3rd MSS
1961-64	3rd MSS Trials of OSBORN combined sweep
1964-1978	3rd MSS based Portland. MCM Trials
Jun 79-Jul 81	Joined 10th MCMS for London Div RNR, based Chatham
Jul-Dec 81	Static tender to London Div RNR berthed Embankment

Significant Events:

Dec 59	Badly damaged in a gale alongside in Gibraltar. Crew commissioned FLORISTON in record time
Nov 72	HRH Prince Charles joined GLASSERTON for 2 weeks MCM experience while serving in HMS MINERVA
Spring 81	Badly damaged in berthing incident at Ramsgate

Paid Off:	July 1981
Disposal:	11 Dec 87 Sold to Pounds then Andover Shipping Broken up by San Esteban de Pravia, Spain
TCA Historian's Note:	Present Record is very sparse. We would welcome any information on GLASSERTON's movements and activities between 1955 and 1979

Laid Down:	14th October 1953
Built by:	Cook, Welton & Gemmell, Beverley North Yorkshire
Completed:	2nd November 1955
Time to Build:	25 Months
Commissioned:	13th March 1955 for 108th Minesweeping Squadron (MSS) based Malta:
Years Fully Operational:	3 months

Outline of Operational Career:

14 Mar 56	Sailed for Malta with KELLINGTON and TARLTON
24 Mar 56	Arrived Malta. Dockyard for Repairs
Jun 56	Crew transferred to ESSINGTON
Jun-Dec 56	Refit Malta then ferry crew to UK. To reserve.

Significant Events:

21-23 Mar 56	Met severe gale (Force 9, gusting 11) off Cape Bon. Severe damage to propellor shaft glands requiring prolonged Dockyard assistance.

Paid Off:	Jun 1956
Disposal:	Dec 1969. Sold to Malaysia as KD LEDANG

HMS HICKLETON

Laid Down:	11th January 1954
Built by:	J I Thornycroft, Woolston
Completed:	24th June 1955
Time to Build:	18 Months
Commissioned:	23rd July 1955 for 108th Minesweeping Squadron (MSS) based Malta
Years Fully Operational:	3

Outline of Operational Career:

9 Sep 55	Joined 108th MSS for passage to Malta
20 Sep 55	Arrived Malta
17 Nov 55	Sailed Malta for First Cyprus Patrol
May-Jul 56	2nd Cyprus Patrol
Nov 56	Took part in Operation MUSKETEER (See illustration above - sweeping in the Suez Canal)
Nov-Dec 56	3rd Cyprus Patrol
Feb-Mar 57	4th Cyprus Patrol
1958	5th & 6th Cyprus Patrols
Feb 59	Paid off in Malta (Crew to UK to man BURNASTON)
1960	Passage to Singapore (Ferry Crew) for Reserve Fleet
10 Apr 65	Commissioned as HMNZS HICKLETON for 11th MCMS
15 Oct-5 Dec 66	Passage to UK via Suez Canal with PICTON

Significant Events:

05-06 Nov 56	Operation MUSKETEER as Influence Sweeper.
17 Nov 56	One of 3 Tons to sweep Suez Canal to 30 km mark
Sep-Nov 58	Short deployment through Suez Canal to Aqaba, Aden, Berbera and Djibouti during period of tension
1965-66	Manned by RNZN during Confrontation Patrols Last ship to engage in gun action in Confrontation.

Paid Off:	December 66
Disposal:	28 Apr 67 Purchased by Argentinian Navy as NEUQUEN

Laid Down:	21st January 1953
Built by:	J I Thorneycroft, Southampton
Completed:	21st May 1955
Time to Build:	28 months (First Deltic Ton)
Commissioned:	21st May 1955 for 105th Minesweeping Squadron (MSS) based Harwich
Years Fully Operational:	18

Outline of Operational Career:

9 Aug 55	Joined 105th MSS at Harwich
Aug-Sep 56	Escorted Inshore Minesweepers to Malta
Oct-Nov 56	Escorted Inshore Minesweepers to UK
1957	Long Refit at Chatham
1958-59	50th Minesweeping (Trials) Squadron at Port Edgar
Nov 59	50th Minesweeping (Trials) Squadron moved to Portland
1 Oct 62	50th MSS renamed 3rd MSS.
Jan-Apr 65	Crew commissioned CARHAMPTON in Aden Emergency.
1972	In Reserve at Gibraltar. Commissioned for FPS in Oct.
1973-1976	Fishery Protection Squadron based Port Edgar

Significant Events:

23 Aug 55	Visited Copenhagen to demonstrate Deltic Engine
Oct 55	Suffered 5 funnel fires on passage Brest to Harwich
5 Oct 56	Major Funnel Fire approaching Taranto.
Oct 56	Withdrawn from Operation MUSKETEER

Paid Off:	3rd March 1976
Disposal:	20 Feb 78 Sold to Tees Marine Services, Middlesborough for break up.

HMS HODGESTON

Laid Down:	September 1952
Built by:	Fleetlands Shipyard Ltd, Gosport
Completed:	17th December 1954
Time to Build:	28 months
Commissioned:	1st February 1955 for 101st (RNR) Minesweeping Squadron based Newcastle
Years Fully Operational:	30

Outline of Operational Career:

1 Feb 1955	Transferred to Tyne Division RNVR as NORTHUMBRIA
1960	Paid off on relief by QUAINTON
Feb 1962	Transferred to Severn Division as VENTURER
1 Jan 76	Reverted to HODGESTON. Allocated SW Group.
1978-1984	Transferred to 10th MCM Squadron NW Group
1985	10th MCM Squadron based Tyne
1985-86	Attached Fishery Protection Squadron

Significant Events:

30 May 55	In collision with MV 'Cyprian Prince' off Longstones Lt. Sustained severe damage. Towed to Tyne for repairs.
20 Sep 76	Involved in search for survivors of HMS FITTLETON

Paid Off:	28 Jul 86
Disposal :	23 Nov 88 Brugse Scheepssloperij, Bruges for break up

Laid Down:	3rd February 1956
Built by:	Camper & Nicholson, Gosport
Completed:	6th June 1958
Time to Build:	28 months
Commissioned:	18th September 1958 for 108th Minesweeping Squadron (MSS) based Malta
Years Fully Operational:	11

Outline of Operational Career:

29 Sep-9 Oct 58	Passage to Malta
25 Oct-4 Nov 58	Deployed to Aqaba to cover withdrawal of British Troops from Jordan
22 Jan-10 Mar 59	First Cyprus Patrol (Stand-off Beirut)
9 Sep 59	Transferred to 104th MSS as Senior Officer
21 Oct-30 Nov 59	Passage to Singapore with WOODBRIDGE HAVEN
1960-61	Exercises and Visits in South China Sea
May & Aug 61	Anti-Piracy Patrols off North Borneo
Dec 61-Jul 63	Confrontation Patrols-Brunei & Sarawak
1964	5 patrols in Sarawak and 2 in Singapore Straits
1965	11 Singapore Straits patrols, 1 Sarawak & 1 Tawau
1966	3 Singapore Straits patrols, 2 Sarawak &1 Tawau

1967-Jun 1969	Exercises and Visits in S. China Sea Area
Jul-Dec 1969	Return to UK eastabout with WILKIESTON (via Darwin, New Guinea, Solomon Islands (4 visits), Vanuata (5 visits), Fiji (14 visits), Tonga, Tarawa, Pearl Harbour, California (3 visits), Mexico, Panama Canal, Jamaica, Bermuda, Azores, Oporto, UK (22,000 miles in 5½ months)

Significant Events:

14-20 Apr 1961	Live Mine Clearance Operation off North Borneo
Apr-May 63	Embarked 60 Gurkhas & 2 Landrovers at Kapit for 160 mile passage down River Rajang to Kuching
11 Feb 65	Arrest of one Fishing craft in Singapore Straits

Paid Off: 22nd December 1969

Disposal: 29th January 1971 Bought by Kitson Vickers, Fleetwood for break up.

Laid Down: 29th January 1953

Built by: Fleetlands Shipyard, Gosport

Completed: 14th October 1955

Time to Build: 32 months

Commissioned: 18th December 1964 for 11th Minesweeping Squadron (MSS) based Singapore

Converted to Minehunter: May 1963 to December 1964 at Chatham

Years Fully Operational: 24

Outline of Operational Career:

Jan-May 65	Work-up in UK Waters
May-Jul 65	Passage to Singapore
1 Jul 1965	Joined 11th MSS. 2 Singapore Straits Patrols
Sep-Dec 65	6 Singapore Straits Patrol (each 5-10 days)
Jan-Aug 66	2 Singapore Straits Patrol (each 10 Days) 1 Sarawak Patrol (12 days) 1 Tawau (N. Borneo) patrol 18 days
1967-9	Exercises & Visits in South China Sea, and Japan
25 Aug 69	6th MCMS transferred to Hong Kong as 6th PBS
Aug 69-Sep 71	Part of 6th Patrol Boat Squadron based Hong Kong

Oct-Dec 71	Returned to UK round Africa
1 Jan 72	Joined newly formed 2nd MCMS based Portsmouth
1973	Period in SNFC
1974-84	2nd MCMS based Portsmouth
Mar 84-Jun 85	Long Refit Rosyth
1985-1988	2nd MCMS based Portsmouth
1 Jan 89	Transferred to 3rd MCMS based Portsmouth
Oct-Nov 89	Exercise TRIDENTE 89 – 3rd MCMS Deployment to Med

Significant Events:

24 Nov 89	Collision with IVESTON while unberthing at Ibiza

Paid Off: 21st February 1991

Disposal: 13th May 1992 Brugse Scheepssloperij, Bruges for BU

HMS ILMINGTON

Laid Down:	24th December 1952
Built by:	Camper & Nicholson Ltd, Gosport
Completed:	5th January 1955
Time to Build:	24 months
Commissioned:	12th February 1955 for 105th Minesweeping Squadron (MSS) based Harwich
Years Fully Operational (RN):	2

Outline of Operational Career:

22 Feb 55	Joined 105th MSS based at Harwich
1955-56	Exercises and visits in Home Waters
Paid Off:	1957
Disposal:	19 Jul 68. Sold to Argentina as 'FORMOSA' (M6)

HMS INVERMORISTON

Pennant No. M1150

Laid Down:	3rd November 1952
Built by:	Dorset Yacht Company, Poole
Completed:	20th January 1955
Time to Build:	26 months
Commissioned:	28th April 1955 for 104th Minesweeping Squadron (MSS) based Harwich
Years Fully Operational:	3

Outline of Operational Career:

4 May 55	Joined 104th MSS at Harwich
1955-56	Exercises and Visits in Home Waters
18 Jul 56	Paid off to Reserve at Hythe. Crew to BURNASTON
1957-63	Operational Reserve at Hythe. Arked.
Mar 63-Mar 64	Refit at Chatham
Aug-Sep 64	Towed to Singapore with PICTON as Theatre Reserve
30 Jan 65	Commissioned for 11th MSS. Crew ex-WISTON
1965	Completed 12 Singapore Straits Patrols (Av. 9 days each) Completed 1 Period Sarawak Patrol (21 Days)
1966	Completed 1 North Borneo Patrol (19 days) Completed 1 Sarawak Patrol (21 days)
17 Sep-5 Nov	Passage to UK with SANTON via Suez Canal

Significant Events:

25 Mar 65	Engaged in firefight with Sampan in Singapore Strait
29 Mar 65	Engaged in firefight with 2 craft in Singapore Strait. One craft sunk but Midshipman Michael O'Driscoll killed.

Paid Off:	Nov 1966
Disposal:	2nd July 1971 by Cashmore of Newport for break up.

Laid Down:	20th October 1952
Built by:	Philip & Sons, Dartmouth
Completed:	29th June 1955
Time to Build:	34 months
Commissioned:	16th October 1964 for 1st Minehunting Squadron based Port Edgar
Years Fully Operational:	28
Conversion:	January 1963 to August 1964 at Devonport – to Minehunter with Deltics

Outline of Operational Career:

13 Nov 64	Arrived Port Edgar
1964-1970	Minehunting Tasks, Exercises and Visits-Home Waters
29 Mar 71	Transferred to 3rd MCMS based Portland
Apr 72	Transferred to 2nd MCMS based at Portsmouth
1973-81	Type 193M Trials, Exercises and Visits
1982-	Type 2093 & Sidescan Sonar Trials
Oct 82-Jan 84	Long Refit at Rosyth
Jul-Aug 84	MSSA 2 sweep trials.
May-Jul 85	Deployment to Mediterranean, inc Toulon
1 Jan 89	Transferred to 3rd MCMS based at Portsmouth
Oct-Nov 89	3rd MCM Deployment to Mediterranean inc Palma
Feb-May 91	Attached to STANAVFORCHAN in Mediterranean
1 Oct 91	Lent to Fishery Protection Squadron

Significant Events:

Feb & May 68	Operation NEW BROOM – Live Mine Clearance Den Helder to Borkum
10 Jun 76	Carried out 19 Op. GRENADA Boardings in one day
19 Apr 80	Bows badly damaged in berthing incident at Portland
1982	IVESTON won Plessey Mine warfare Trophy
17 Mar 84	GAVINTON collided with IVESTON amidships during Team Sweep – Limited damage
1989	IVESTON won Plessey Mine warfare Trophy
24 Oct 89	Damaged by HUBBERSTON during unberthing at Ibiza
1992	IVESTON won Plessey Mine warfare Trophy

Paid Off: 21st July 1992

Disposal: 28th August 1993 to Sea Cadets, Tilbury as HQ Ship

HMS KEDLESTON

Pennant No. M1153

Laid Down:	26th November 1952
Built by:	William Pickersgill, Sunderland
Completed:	2nd July 1955
Time to Build:	32 Months
Commissioned:	23rd January 1969 for Fishery Protection Squadron (FPS) based Port Edgar
Years Fully Operational:	21
Conversion:	to Deltic Engined Minehunter at Devonport 1967-1969

Outline of Operational Career:

April 1969	Joined FPS at Port Edgar
1969-1973	Fishery Protection Patrols
7 Jan 74	Transferred to Forth Div RNR as first RNR Minehunter
13 Jan 75	Reverted to FPS
01 Jan 76	Transferred to 10th MCMS, North East Group
Oct 79-Jul 80	Major Refit at Gibraltar

Aug 1980	Rejoined 10th MCMS for Forth Division
Apr-Jun 82	Deployment to Catania & Lisbon for NATO Exercises
Oct 86	Transferred to 3rd MCMS based Rosyth
15 May 88	Transferred to Fishery Protection Squadron
Dec 88-1991	Transferred to Northern Ireland Squadron. Multiple (14) Grenada patrols. No mine hunting capability.

Significant Events:

4 Sep 75	Arrested 10 foreign fishing trawlers in single day off North Yorkshire coast. All skippers convicted and fined.
9 Sep 88	Serious fire onboard. Repairs took two months.

Paid Off: 1991

Disposal: 20 April 1992 – To Bruges, Belgium for breaking up

HMS KELLINGTON Pennant No. M1154

Laid Down:	6th January 1954
Built by:	William Pickersgill & Co Ltd, Sunderland
Completed:	4th November 1955
Time to Build:	22 Months
Commissioned:	8th March 1956 for 108th Minesweeping Squadron (MSS) based Malta
Years Fully Operational:	22
Conversion:	to Deltic Engined Minehunter at Chatham July 1967 to June 1969

Outline of Operational Career:

24 Mar 56	Joined 108th MSS at Malta
1 Apr-18 Jun 56	Cyprus Patrol (3 periods with port visits between)
30 Jun 56	Left Malta for UK
11 Jul 56	Reduced to Reserve at Hythe
06 Jun 69	Recommissioned at Chatham for FPS
31 Jul 69	Joined Fishery Protection Squadron at Port Edgar
1969-1976	FP Patrols and Minehunting exercises
16 Nov 76	Transferred to Sussex RNR based at Shoreham
21 Jul-24 Aug 77	Deep Water Minesweeping Trials off Gibraltar
1982	Long Refit at Rosyth
1 Apr 85	Reverted to 3rd MCMS from RNR Service.
11 Jan-31 Jul 88	Attached to STANAVFORCHAN
Jun 89-Sep 92	On loan to FPS

Significant Events:

17 Nov 73	Stood by MV CAP ANTONIO on fire off Dover.
4 Jan 74	Stood by drifting leg of Oil Rig in Storm Force 12 NE of Shetlands. Suffered upper deck damage.
30 Jun 75	Stood by FV 'Blackendene' on fire off Shetlands.
01 Aug 84	First RNR ship to win Plessey MCM Efficiency Trophy.
24 Feb 91	Stood by MV BREDON MERCHANT on fire off Sussex

Paid Off: 24th September 1992

Disposal: 1993-2007 Lent to Stockton on Tees Sea Cadet Unit as HQ Ship
June 2009 Broken up in situ.

Laid Down:	21st January 1953
Built by:	Harland & Wolff Ltd, Belfast
Completed:	21st May 1954
Time to Build:	16 Months
Commissioned:	8th June 1962 for 9th Minesweeping Squadron (MSS) based Aden
Years Fully Operational:	4

Outline of Operational Career:

27 Aug-10 Sep 62	Passage to Malta alone (delayed by defects)
11 to 28 Sep 62	Work up at Malta
29 Sep-8 Oct 62	Passage to Aden
Jan-Mar 63	Preliminary deployment to Persian Gulf
1 May 63	9th MSS moved permanently to Bahrain
1963-66	Patrols, exercises and visits in Persian Gulf, change crew and recommission annually in Oct
Oct-Nov 66	Passage to UK

Significant Events:

20 Feb 63	KEMERTON collided with FLOCKTON during Night Minesweeping Exercise. Both ships seaworthy.

Paid Off:	23rd November 1966
Disposal:	25th October 1971 Sold to Solent Power Boats, thence to Pounds Portsmouth for break up at Poole.

HMS KILDARTON Pennant No. M1162

Laid Down:	30th July 1954
Built by:	Harland & Wolff
Completed:	25th November 1955
Time to Build:	16 months
Commissioned:	January 1956 for 108th Minesweeping Squadron (MSS) based Malta
Years Fully Operational:	4

Outline of Operational Career:

5 Jul–14 Jul 56	Passage to Malta to Join 108th MSS
Jul-Nov 56	Cyprus Patrols
6 Nov-12 Nov 56	Operation MUSKETEER. At Port Said
Dec 1956	Transferred to 104th MSS
1957-59	At Malta and Cyprus Patrols
16 Mar 59	Paid off to Reserve Malta
Oct 1960	Towed to Singapore for Reserve Fleet, Far East
17 May 65	Commissioned for 11th Minesweeping Squadron
1965-66	Singapore Straits and Borneo Patrols
12-31 May 66	Passage to Aden
22 Mar 67	Arrived Portsmouth to pay off

Significant Events:

05-06 Nov 56	Took part in Operation MUSKETEER - Wire then Influence Sweeper

Paid Off:	April 1967
Disposal:	September 1969. Sold for Conversion to Oil Rig Supply Ship.

HMS KIRKLISTON

Laid Down:	3rd February 1953
Built by:	Harland & Wolff
Completed:	21st August 1954
Time to Build:	18 Months
Transferred:	25th October 1954 to 101st (RNVR) MSS as HMS KILMOREY based Belfast
Conversion:	to Minehunter at Chatham December 1962 to September1964
Years Fully Operational:	26 years

Outline of Operational Career:

25 Oct 54	Arrived Belfast as tender to Ulster RNR
1954-1960	Home waters as RNR Ulster Tender
Aug 1960	Reverted to RN. Conversion to Deltic Engines.
7 May 1962	Commissioned for 50th MSS based Portland
1 Oct 1962	50th MSS renamed 3rd MSS
22 Nov 62	Decommissioned for conversion at Chatham
Oct 1964	Joined 1st Minehunting Squadron at Port Edgar as SO
1966	Joined 6th MSS based Singapore
1970	Moved base to Hong Kong
22 May 72	Sailed for UK – arrived Portsmouth 29 Aug 72, then transferred to 1st MCMS at Lochinvar
Oct 73-Oct 74	Long Refit at Gibraltar (No Ships Company)
1974-1982	Transferred to 10th MCMS for Forth Division. 1st RNR M/H
1983-1985	Allocated to 2nd MCMS based Portsmouth

Significant Events:

18 Jul 67	Holed below waterline while recovering a steel US aircraft bombing target. 3 months repairs at Singapore.
Sep-Oct 68	Deployment to NE Australia (Mackay & Cairns)
Oct-Dec 84	Operation HARLING in Red Sea
Paid Off:	5th December 1985
Disposal:	20 Oct 91 to Brugse Scheepssloperji, Bruges, for break up

Laid Down:	12th March 1953
Built by:	Harland & Wolff
Completed:	10th November 1954
Time to Build:	20 months
Commissioned:	January 1955 for VERNON Training Squadron (with BILDESTON Crew)
Conversion:	To Diving Trials Ship 1966-1967
Years Fully Operational:	22

Outline of Operational Career:

Jan 55	Joined VERNON Training Squadron
1956	Refit and defect rectification (Four COs in year)
Oct 60	Paid off for Deltic Conversion (prolonged)
1961-62	Refit and reserve
Jan 63	Recommissioned as SO of 3rd MSS based Portland.
Jan 65	Paid Off to reserve. Crew to Aden to man CALTON.
7 Mar 67	Recommissioned as Diving Trials ship
1967-71	Diving Trials and visits in North European Waters .

Oct-Nov 71	Deployment to Mediterranean
1971-78	Diving trials and training
Nov 78- 82	10th MCMS – NW Sea Training Group

Significant Events:

17 Nov 59	Took 10 Admirals to sea for the day.
30 Jun 68	Escorted yacht 'Lively Lady' (Sir Alec Rose) up Channel
28 Jun 77	Participated in Spithead Review
Apr 1978	Participated in AMOCO CADIZ clean up

Paid Off: February 1982

Disposal: 26th February 1985. Sold to G & T Services, Barking for breaking up

Laid Down:	27th November 1953
Built by:	Harland & Wolff, Belfast
Completed:	10th March 1955
Time to Build:	16 months
Commissioned:	25th April 1955 as Air Training Target Ship based Devonport
Years Fully Operational:	6 Years

Outline of Operational Career:

1955-56	Air Training Target Ship, Plymouth
1957	Refit (Sheathing) then Reserve at Hythe
Oct 1958	Towed to Aden by Tug CAUTIOUS, then Reserve
Jul 1961	Commissioned at Aden. Passage to Singapore
23 Apr 62	Recommissioned for service with 120th MSS
16 May 62	Arrived at new base port Hong Kong.
1 Oct 62	120th MSS renamed 8th MSS
1964-1966	Carried out 10 patrols off Tawau, Sabah
Jan-Mar 67	Returned to UK with DUFTON & PENSTON

Significant Events:

Sep 64	Hit by Indonesian shell off Sabah
23 Mar 65	Ran aground off Tawau and lost propellor. Towed back to Hong Kong by RFA GOLD RANGER

Paid Off:	May 1967
Disposal:	4th April 1970. Sold to Bakkerzonen of Bruges for BU

HMS LETTERSTON   Pennant No. M1160

Laid Down:	18th February 1954
Built by:	Harland & Wolff, Belfast
Completed:	29th June 1955
Time to Build:	16 months
Commissioned:	July 1955 for 104th Minesweeping Squadron (MSS) based Harwich
Years Fully Operational:	6 Years

Outline of Operational Career:

July 1955	Joined 104th MSS at Harwich, vice BEVINGTON
1955-56	Exercises, and Home and N. European Visits
Aug-Sep 56	Passage to Malta for Op MUSKETEER
28 Oct 56	Cyprus Patrol
4-12 Nov 56	Operation MUSKETEER
14 Nov-Dec 56	Cyprus Patrol
17-28 Jan 57	Passage to UK to pay off to Reserve at Chatham
1957-1964	Reserve Fleet, Hythe
24 Feb 64	Recommissioned for CinC Plymouth
Oct 64	Joined Fishery Protection Squadron at Port Edgar
1964-68	Fishery Protection Squadron

Significant Events:

5-6 Nov 56	Took part in Operation MUSKETEER as Danlayer
Jan-Jun 65	Arrested 4 Foreign Trawlers. All Convicted
Jan-Aug 66	Arrested 6 Foreign Trawlers. All Convicted
Jul 68	Escorted Yacht 'LIVELY LADY' up Channel
Nov-Dec 68	Arrested 4 Foreign Trawlers. All Convicted.

Paid Off:	Aug 1969
Disposal:	9th June 1971 Sold to C H Rugg to be scrapped in Belgium

HMS LEVERTON

HMS Leverton at anchor off the residence of the redoubtable Rear Admiral Miers VC,
Flag Officer Middle East, Cyprus. 1957 - Photograph Courtesy Edward Booker

Laid Down: 18th May 1954

Built by: Harland & Wolff, Belfast

Completed: 25th August 1955

Time to Build: 15 months

Commissioned: 3rd September 1955 for 108th Minesweeping Squadron (MSS) based Malta

Years Fully Operational: 12

Outline of Operational Career:

11Oct-4 Nov 55	Passage to Malta via Gibraltar & Bizerta
1956	3 Periods Cyprus Patrol, Exercises & Visits
1957	3 Periods Cyprus Patrol, Exercises & Visits
21 Nov-2 Dec 57	Passage to UK. Paid off for Deltic Conversion
Mar 58-May 59	Deltic Conversion at Plymouth
Jun 59	Recommissioned for 108th MSS based Malta
8-17 Jul 59	Passage to Malta.
Aug 59-Jan 60	Three periods Cyprus Patrol
1960-1969	Exercises and Visits in Mediterranean
31 Mar 69	7th MSS were last RN ships to leave Malta

Significant Events:

5-6 Nov 56	Took part in Operation MUSKETEER as Wire Sweeper
Jul-Sep 61	Deployment to Aden & Bahrain for Kuwait Emergency

Paid Off: April 1969

Disposal: 13th August 1971 to Pounds for scrapping

HMS LEWISTON

Laid Down:	19th October 1956
Built by:	Herd & Mackenzie, Buckie, Banff
Completed:	16th June 1960
Time to Build:	45 months
Commissioned:	30th August 1960 as Senior Officer 100th Minesweeping Squadron (MSS)
Years Fully Operational:	23 years

Outline of Operational Career:

Sep 1960	Joined 100th MSS at Port Edgar
1961-62	Exercises and Visits in North European waters
1 Oct 62	100th MSS renamed 2nd MSS
1963	WWII Mine Clearance Operations (See below)
1964	Exercisers and Visits in North European waters
18 Jan 65	Paid Off to Reserve, Crew to Singapore for PICTON
21 Jun 65	Recommissioned in 1st MCMS at Port Edgar. New Crew
1965-1971	Exercises and Visits in North European waters
Mar 1972	Joined 2nd MCMS based Portsmouth

1981-May 83	Joined 10th MCMS RNR Squadron as London Div Tender
May 83	Rejoined 2nd MCMS

Significant Events:

May-Jul 63	Took part in Operations CLEAR ROAD and CABLE WAY. Clearance of WWII German minefields to allow new telegraph cables to be laid from the UK to Germany.
Sep 1963	Took part in Operation ICE SCOTT – Clearance of British anti-submarine minefields in approaches to Icelandic fjords.

Paid Off: January 1984

Disposal: 1985 - Expended as a target on Aberforth Ranges

Laid Down:	26th October 1954
Built by:	Harland & Wolff, Belfast
Completed:	1st June 1956
Time to Build:	20 months
Commissioned:	8th December 1956 for 104th Minesweeping Squadron (MSS) based Malta
Years Fully Operational:	2 1/2

Outline of Operational Career:

Jan 1957	Passage to Malta. Joined 104th MSS
1957-Jul 58	Completed 4 periods of Cyprus Patrol
Aug-Sep 58	Deployed to Aden for 3 weeks
Nov 1958	Cyprus Patrol
Dec 1958	Paid off to Reserve in Malta
Jan-Feb 1960	Passage (Ferry Crew) to Singapore
Mar 60-Dec 64	Station Reserve in Singapore
20 Jan 1965	Commissioned for 11th MCMS. Singapore Straits Patrols

Significant Events:

26 Mar 65	Challenged a sampan off Johore, and two occupants immediately jumped overboard
Paid Off:	17th May 1965
Disposal:	1966 Transferred to Royal Malaysian Navy as KD TAHAN

HMS MARYTON

Laid Down:	24th November 1955
Built by:	Montrose Shipyard
Completed:	13th November 1958
Time to Build:	36 months
Commissioned:	20th January 1959 for 104th Minesweeping Squadron (MSS) based Malta
Years Fully Operational:	8

Outline of Operational Career:

19-27 Feb 59	Passage to Malta to join 104th MSS
1959	Completed 2 Cyprus Patrols
Nov-Dec 59	Deployed to Singapore to rejoin 104th MSS
1960-1962	Exercises and visits in South China Sea
1963	Completed 6 North Borneo Patrols (av.3 weeks each)
1964	4 Borneo & 1 Straits Patrol
1965	11 periods Straits Patrol (each 2 weeks) and 3 off Borneo
1966	1 Straits Patrol and 2 Borneo Patrols
Oct-Dec 67	Returned to UK round Africa alone

Significant Events:

8-29 Aug 62	Anti-piracy patrol off Borneo with CHAWTON
Aug & Oct 63	Hit submerged log. Lost large areas of sheathing; Damaged starboard propeller 7 Oct
7 Dec 66	Grounded during Exercise off Sabah. Pulled off by WOODBRIDGE HAVEN. 5 month refit ensued

Paid Off:	January 1968
Disposal:	5th July 1969. Sold for disposal. Broken up at Cairnryan

HMS MAXTON Pennant No. M1165

Laid Down: 23rd May 1955

Built by: Harland & Wolff, Belfast

Completed: 19 February 1957

Time to Build: 21 Months

Commissioned: 4th July 1958 for 104th Minesweeping Squadron (MSS) based Malta (PENSTON crew)

Conversion: to Deltic Engined Minehunter at Devonport 1964 to March 1966

Years Fully Operational: 27 years

Outline of Operational Career:

Jul 58	Deployed to Malta.
24 Jan 59	Damage Repair Malta. Ships Company to SANTON.
25 Jun 59	Recommissioned for 104th MSS.
01 Oct 59	Transferred to 108th MSS
1958-1961	9 Cyprus Patrols. Damaged in collision with HMS UNDAUNTED
Apr 62	Paid off at Devonport. Reserve at Hythe.
11 Mar 66	Recommissioned as Minehunter for Far East
30Jun-26 Aug 66	Passage to Singapore. Joined 6th MCMS (1 Nov 66)
1966-69	Exercises and Visits in South China Sea
25 Aug 69	6th MCMS became 6th Patrol Craft Squadron (PCS)
13 Oct 69	Joined 6th PCS based Hong Kong
1969-71	Local Exercises and Patrols based Hong Kong
Oct-Dec 71	Passage to UK on relief by YARNTON
1972-73	Long Refit Rosyth, then joined 1st MCMS Port Edgar
Mar-Nov 74	Operation RHEOSTAT–Clear Explosives Suez Canal
1975-83	Operations and Exercises in UK Waters, except:

Jul 78	Deployment to Gibraltar for EDATS Trials
Aug-Sep 79	Deployment to Portugal & Spain with 1st MCMS
1 Jan 84	Transferred to newly formed 3rd MCMS based Rosyth
Apr to Jun 84	Deployment to Mediterranean (Corfu) with SHERATON
Mar 85-Mar 86	Transferred temporarily to Sussex Div RNR

Significant Events:

24 Dec 58	Collision with HMS UNDAUNTED south of Larnaca, Cyprus. Damage Starboard side above waterline.
Sep-Oct 68	Deployment to Australia for Exercises with RAN
15 Jun 74	First ship to pass through Suez Canal since 1967
25-30 Sep 76	Involved in FITTLETON Salvage Operations
Apr-Sep 82	CO and Crew members transferred to STUFT Trawlers for deployment to Falklands

Paid Off: 19th August 1988

Disposal: 17th April 1989: Sold for Break-up by Franciscomata SA at El Ferrol.

HMS MONKTON

Laid Down:	16th December 1953
Built by:	Herd & Mackenzie, Buckie, Banff
Completed:	27th February 1957
Time to Build:	38 Months
Commissioned:	April 1959 for Vernon Training Squadron (VTS) based Portsmouth
Conversion:	to Patrol Vessel at Devonport for service in Hong Kong September & October 1971
Years Fully Operational:	26

Outline of Operational Career:

May 1959	Arrived Portsmouth to join Vernon Squadron
1960-1965	Local exercises, and visits in N European waters
1 Oct 1962	Vernon Training Squadron renamed 5th MSS
Dec 1965	Transferred to 1st MCMS based Port Edgar
1966-1968	Exercises and visits in North European waters
1 Jan 69	Transferred to Plymouth Command for SAR duties
1 Sep 71	Conversion to Patrol Craft at Devonport.
Jan-Apr 72	Passage to Hong Kong in company
1972-85	Hong Kong Patrol Craft Squadron as P1055

Significant Events:

Nov 62-Jul 63	Ships Company transferred to THAMES, then BEACHAMPTON due long term shaft defects
May 1968	Operation NEW BROOM based Borkum
Sep 1971	Conversion to Patrol Craft- Additional Bofors and Machine guns; some armour plating: Minesweeping gear removed

Paid Off:	17th April 1985
Disposal:	23rd May 1985. Sold to Hing Fat Metal Co for break up at Hong Kong.

HMS NURTON

Laid Down:	31st August 1955
Built by:	Harland & Wolff, Belfast
Completed:	21st August 1957
Time to Build:	24 months
Commissioned:	November 1957 for 101st (RNVR) Minesweeping Squadron (MSS) based Dundee
Conversion:	to Deltic-engined Minehunter at Portsmouth September 1964 to December 1965
Years Fully Operational:	33

Outline of Operational Career:

Nov 57-Oct 60	Allocated to Tay Division RNR
Oct 60-Dec 61	Deltic Conversion at Portsmouth
Dec 61-Oct 62	Transferred to Vernon Squadron at Portsmouth
1 Oct 1962	Vernon Squadron renamed 5th MSS
10 Jul 64	Transferred to FO Plymouth for SAR duties
Sep 64-Dec 65	Minehunter Conversion at Portsmouth
2 Feb 66	Joined 1st MCMS at Port Edgar as SO
1966-73	Exercises and Visits in North European Waters
3 Sep 74	Transferred to 2nd MCMS based Portsmouth
1974-82	Exercises and Visits in North European Waters
1981 & 1982	Attached to STANAVFORCHAN Jan-Jun
May 83-Jul 84	Repairs and major refit at Rosyth
1984-88	Exercises and Visits in North European Waters
1989	Refit and Conversion for Northern Ireland Patrol
1990-1993	Allocated to Northern Ireland Patrol Squadron

Significant Events:

9-11 May 58	Largest warship to navigate Tay up to Perth for visit.
6-30 May 68	Operation NEW BROOM (Live M/S) off Den Helder
19-28 Sep 69	Lifesaving and salvage at Gothenburg after storm
24 Feb 83	Collision with BROCKLESBY in fog off Portland. Holed amidships. Towed to Rosyth for repairs

Paid Off: 3rd December 1993 Last operational TON in the Royal Navy

Disposal: 21st June 1995 via Pounds for break up by Dawn Premier Service,Selby

HMS PENSTON Pennant No. M1169

Laid Down:	16th July 1954
Built by:	Cook, Welton & Gemmell Ltd, Beverley, Yorks
Completed:	9th March 1956
Time to Build:	20 months
Commissioned:	24th August 1956 for 108th Minesweeping Squadron (MSS) based Malta
Years Fully Operational:	8

Outline of Operational Career:

24 Aug-4 Sep 56	Passage to Malta (with ALDINGTON)
25 Sep-12 Nov 56	First Cyprus Patrol (71 days)
14 Nov-21 Dec 56	At Port Said as Op MUSKETEER relief
Jun 58	Paid off at Malta. (Crew to UK to man MAXTON).
Oct 58	Refit, then reserve at Malta
1959	Towed to Aden. Reserve Fleet Aden.
Oct-Nov 61	Towed to Singapore. Far East Reserve
26 Apr 62	Commissioned for 120th MSS based Hong Kong
1 Oct 62	120th MSS renamed 8th MSS
1962-1963	Immigration Patrols in disputed waters
1964	82 days North Borneo (Tawau) Patrols
1965	119 days North Borneo (Tawau) Patrols
1966	36 days North Borneo Patrols
Feb-Apr 67	Returned to UK to decommission

Significant Events:

6 Mar 57	Night collision with ALDINGTON off Sardinia.
5 Sep 64	Present when Typhoon Ruby hit Hong Kong.

Paid Off:	April 1967
Disposal:	28th January 1970 Sold to Metrec, Newhaven for breaking up.

Laid Down:	27th January 1955
Built by:	Cook, Welton & Gemmell Ltd, Beverley, Yorks
Completed:	19th July 1956
Time to Build:	18 months
Commissioned:	20th January 1965 as Senior Officer 11th Minecountermeasures Squadron (MCMS) based Singapore
Years Fully Operational:	2

Outline of Operational Career:

1965	36 days Borneo & 115 Days Singapore Straits Patrol
Jan 1966	17 days Singapore Straits Patrol
May-Aug 66	Exercises and Visits in South China Sea
Oct-Dec 66	Passage to UK with HICKLETON via Suez Canal.

Significant Events:

26 May 05	Intercepted sampan in Singapore Straits. High speed chase. Sampan blew up when fired on.

Paid Off:	December 1966
Disposal:	28th July 1969 Sold to SB Queenborough at Cairnryan

HMS POLLINGTON

Completed:	5th September 1958
Time to Build:	41 months
Commissioned:	October 1959 for 101st (RNR) Minesweeping Squadron (MSS) as HMS MERSEY based Liverpool
Years Fully Operational:	22 years

Outline of Operational Career:

1960-1975	Weekend and Continuous Training Periods and visits to UK and North European Ports
1962	101st MSS renamed 10th MCMS
1963-1971	Deployments to Gibraltar ('ROCKHAUL/MAINHAUL Series') annually in Aug-Sep (except in 1965,'66 and '68)
Nov 75	Paid off to Reserve
11 Feb 78	Commissioned at Chatham for FPS
1978-85	Fishery Protection Patrols

Significant Events:

Jun 1963	Took part in Operation 'CABLE LAY', a live minesweeping operation based on Borkum.
Feb-Apr 65	Took part in Operation 'STOP GAP', deployment of 3 RNR ships and an RFA to West Indies.
May 1968	Took Part in Operation 'NEW BROOM', live M/S operation based on Borkum.
Aug-Sep 73	Took part in Exercise MAPLEHAUL, RNR Deployment To Canadian East Coast Ports.
3 Aug 79	Embarked King Olav of Norway for day to review Manx Herring Fleet

Paid Off:	28th March 1985
Disposal:	25th March 1987 Sold to SB Queenborough, Cairnryan for break up.

Laid Down:	20th March 1954
Built by:	Richards Ironworks, Lowestoft
Completed:	20th September 1957
Time to Build:	42 months
Commissioned:	23rd April 1959 for 104th Minesweeping Squadron (MSS) based Malta
Years Fully Operational:	11

Outline of Operational Career:

4-14 May 59	Passage to Malta. Joined 104th MSS
6 Jul-11 Aug 59	First (and only) Cyprus Patrol
21 Oct-30 Nov 59	Passage Malta to Singapore with WOODBRIDGE HAVEN and 104th MSS
1960-62	Exercises and Visits in South China Sea
Jun-Dec 62	North Borneo Patrol (26 days)
Oct 1962	104th MSS renumbered 6th MSS
1963	North Borneo Patrol (122 days), exercises & visits
1964	North Borneo Patrol 109 days), exercises & visits
1965	Borneo (57) & Singapore Straits (144 days) Patrol
1966	Borneo(41) & Singapore Straits (19 days) Patrol
Oct 66	Passage to Bahrain. Joined 9th MSS
May-Jul 67	Anti-gun running patrol off Aden & Dhofar
May-Jul 68	Passage Bahrain to Gibraltar for Refit
Mar-May 69	Passage Gibraltar to Bahrain
Jun 69-Aug 71	Exercises and Visits in Gulf Area
5 Sep-18 Nov 71	Passage from Bahrain to UK with WISTON

Significant Events:

28 May 1965   Incident with Indonesian 'Kronstadt' Class Patrol Vessel in Singapore Straits. Guns trained.

Paid Off: 19th November 1971

Disposal :   3rd May 1972 Sold on to Pounds Portsmouth for conversion to survey vessel, then sold on to Henderson Merez, Dartford in 1977 for break up.

Laid Down:	10th March 1955
Built by:	Richards Ironworks, Lowestoft
Completed:	5th February 1959
Time to Build:	47 months
Commissioned:	2nd May 1960 for 101st (RNR) Minesweeping Squadron as HMS NORTHUMBRIA Newcastle
Years Fully Operational:	12 years

Outline of Operational Career:

May 1960	Joined 101st MSS based Newcastle
1960-72	Tyne Division RNR as HMS NORTHUMBRIA
1 Oct 62	101st MSS renamed 10th MSS
Feb-Apr 65	Took part in Operation 'STOP GAP', deployment of 3 RNR ships and an RFA to West Indies.
Aug-Sep 69	To Gibraltar for Exercise ROCKHAUL 69
Aug-Sep 70	To Gibraltar for Exercise MAINHAUL 70
Sep 71	To Gibraltar for Exercise MAINHAUL 71

Significant Events:

24 Jul 60	Ran aground off Holy Island. Refloated
13 Apr 62	Damaged bows while berthing at Gateshead
09 Sep 68	Damaged in collision with WARSASH (BOULSTON)

Paid Off:	August 1972
Disposal:	30th July 1979 Sold to C F Booth at Blyth for breaking up

HMS REPTON

Laid Down:	27th January 1956
Built by:	Harland & Wolff, Belfast
Completed:	11th December 1957
Time to Build:	23 months
Commissioned:	27th August 1962 for Vernon Training Squadron (VTS) based Portsmouth
Years Fully Operational:	11 years

Outline of Operational Career:

25 Sep 62	Joined Vernon Training Squadron
1 Oct 62	Vernon Training Squadron renamed 5th MSS
1963-65	Day running, Exercises and Visits in N. European Waters
Sep 1965	Paid off at Portsmouth for Care and Maintenance
Apr 1967	Towed to Gibraltar for Reserve Fleet
5 Apr 71	Commissioned at Port Edgar for 10th MCMS as CLYDE
16 Apr 71	Clyde Division RNR based Glasgow
Aug-Sep 71	To Gibraltar for Exercise MAINHAUL 71
1972-1975	RNR Training, Fleet Exercises and Visits
1 Jan 76	Reverted to name REPTON. Allocated NW Group RNR
1 Jan 78	Reallocated to NE Group 10th MCMS
1 Jan 79	Loaned to Fishery Protection Squadron

Significant Events:

11-30 May 63	Took part in Operation CLEAR ROAD – Live minesweeping operation off Esjberg, Denmark
20 Aug 76	Present at FITTLETON sinking. Guarded wreck site

Paid Off:	March 1980
Disposal:	16th July 1982 Sold to Pounds of Portsmouth for breaking up

HMS RODINGTON
Pennant No. M1177

Laid Down:	14th July 1953
Built by:	Fleetlands Shipyard, Gosport
Completed:	22nd July 1955
Time to Build:	24 months
Commissioned:	4th August 1955 for 108th Minesweeping Squadron (MSS) based Harwich
Years Fully Operational:	3 years

Outline of Operational Career:

27 Aug 55	Joined 108th MSS at Harwich
9-25 Sep 55	Passage to Malta with 108th MSS
6 Oct-28 Nov 55	First Cyprus Patrol
1956	3 periods Cyprus Patrol
15 Nov-15 Dec 56	At Port Said (after Op. MUSKETEER)
1957	3 Periods Cyprus Patrol
Sep 1957	Returned to UK. Paid off to Reserve 18 Oct.
1959	Towed to Gibraltar
May 1961	Commissioned for 108th MSS vice SHAVINGTON
4 Jul-22 Sep	Deployment to Aden & Bahrain during Kuwait Crisis
Jan-Mar 62	Exercises and Visits in Mediterranean

Paid Off:	26th March 1962
Disposal:	12th May 1972 Kitson Vickers at Fleetwood for break up

HMS SANTON

Pennant No. M1178

Laid Down:	12th April 1954
Built by:	Fleetlands Shipyard, Gosport
Completed:	21st February 1956
Time to Build:	23 months
Commissioned: 1	4th June 1956 as Tender to HMS REDPOLE for Navigation Training, Portsmouth
Years Fully Operational:	9 (RN)

Outline of Operational Career:

Jun-Oct 56	Navigation Training, Portsmouth Areas
19 Oct 56	Paid off at Portsmouth
10 Nov 56	Recommissioned with BADMINTON's Crew.
27 Nov-6 Dec 56	Passage to Malta to join 104th MSS
1957	5 periods of Cyprus Patrol (115 days)
1958	3 periods of Cyprus Patrol (97 days)
19 Aug 58	Paid off to Reserve in Malta.
18 Nov 59	Commissioned for passage to Singapore. Ferry Crew.
Nov 59-Jan 60	Passage to Singapore. To Reserve on arrival.
10 Apr 65	Commissioned with RNZN Crew for 11th MCMS
1965	102 days of Singapore & Malacca Straits Patrol, 43 days of Borneo Patrol.
1966	43 days of Singapore & Malacca Straits Patrol, 22 days of Borneo Patrol. Last Patrol 10 Aug.
Sep-Nov 66	Passage to UK via Suez Canal

Paid Off:	November 1966
Disposal:	18th May 1967 Sold to ARGENTINA as CHABUT

Laid Down:	18th May 1953
Built by:	Whites Shipyard Ltd, Southampton
Completed:	28th June 1955
Time to Build:	25 months
Commissioned:	18th July 1955 as Senior Officer 108th Minesweeping Squadron (MSS) based Malta
Years Fully Operational:	3

Outline of Operational Career:

9-20 Sep 55	Passage to Malta with 108th MSS
30 Sep-19 Dec 55	First Cyprus Patrol (75 Days on patrol)
10 Feb-30 Mar 56	2nd Cyprus Patrol (40 Days on patrol)
24 Nov-20 Dec 56	3rd Cyprus Patrol (26 Days on patrol)
22 Feb-29 Mar 57	4th Cyprus Patrol (36 days on patrol
30 Apr-25 May 57	5th Cyprus Patrol (26 days on patrol)
5 Jul-29 Jul 57	6th Cyprus Patrol (25 days on patrol)
Aug 58	Paid off Malta. Crew UK to commission HOUGHTON
1959-64	Towed to ADEN for Reserve
20 Oct 64	Recommissioned for passage to UK for Refit

Significant Events:

31 Oct-21 Nov 56	Took part in Operation MUSKETEER Docking in FS FOUDRE to change propellers Led sweeping force down canal to 33 km mark - proceeded furthest south before UN took over.

Paid Off:	30th November 1964
Disposal:	2nd July 1968 Sold to CH Rugg. Transferred to Bakkerzonen, Bruges for break up

HMS SHAVINGTON

Pennant No. M1180

Laid Down:	30th September 1953
Built by:	Whites Shipbuilding Co Ltd, Southampton
Completed:	1st March 1956
Time to Build:	29 months
Commissioned:	28th June 1956 for 108th Minesweeping Squadron (MSS) based Malta
Years Fully Operational:	22

Outline of Operational Career:

5-14 Jun 56	Passage to Malta
22 Jul-28 Aug 56	First Cyprus Patrol (34 days)
31 Oct-15 Nov 56	Operation MUSKETEER
20 Nov 56	Recommissioned for 104th MSS
1-14 Jan 57	2nd Cyprus Patrol (14 days)
22 May-6 Jul 57	3rd Cyprus Patrol (46 days)
18 Oct–2 Dec 57	4th Cyprus Patrol (43 days)
27 Dec-3 Jan 58	Returned to UK. Paid off
Apr 58-Jul 59	Deltic Conversion at Portsmouth
13-23 Jul 59	Passage to Malta. Joined 108th MSS
1-28 Aug 59	5th Cyprus Patrol (25 days)
7 Oct-22 Nov 59	6th Cyprus Patrol (42 days)
Sep-Dec 61	Deployment to Aden & Arabian Sea
1 Oct 62	108th MSS renumbered 7th MSS
1962-1968	Exercises and Visits in Mediterranean
31 Mar 69	7th MSS final departure from Malta
Apr 1969	Paid off at Gibraltar to Reserve

11 Oct 74	Commissioned at Devonport for FP Squadron
1975-82	Fishery Protection Patrols
May 1982	Transferred to Ulster Division RNR based Belfast

Significant Events:

5-6 Nov 56	Took part in Operation MUSKETEER - Wire Sweeping
9 May 61	BURNASTON collided with SHAVINGTON on passage SHAVINGTON damaged (replaced by RODINGTON)
28 Jun 77	Took part in Silver Jubilee Revue at Spithead
3-5 Aug 77	Multiple Boardings off North East Coast during Salmon Patrol. Four arrests, one prosecution.
23 Dec 77	Salvaged Greek MV 'Fast Bird II' off St Ives

Paid Off: 18th March 1985

Disposal: 25th March 1987 Sold to SB Queenborough at Cairnryan for break up

HMS SHERATON

Laid Down:	23rd February 1954
Built by:	Whites Shipyard, Itchen, Southampton
Completed: 2	4th August 1956
Time to Build:	30 months
Commissioned:	27th January 1959 for RNR training and for ACR/DNR, based at Portsmouth
Converted:	To Minehunter - 29 June 1964 to 30 Apr 1965, at Portsmouth
Years Fully Operational:	33 years

Outline of Operational Career:

1959-61	RNR Training & Visits in North European waters
24 Feb 62	Joined Vernon Squadron
1 Oct 62	Vernon Squadron renamed 5th MSS
29 Jun 64	Paid Off for Minehunter Conversion
28 Apr 65	Recommissioned at Portsmouth for 6th MCMS
27 Aug-8 Oct 65	Passage to Singapore via South Africa
Oct-Dec 65	Completed 6 Singapore Straits Patrols (47 days)
1967-69	Exercises and Visits in South China Sea
28 Aug 69	Joined 6th Patrol Craft Squadron based Hong Kong
1970-May 72	Exercises & Visits in South China Sea
22 May-24 Aug 72	Passage to UK with KIRKLISTON
1 Sep 72	Joined 1st MCMS based Port Edgar
1973-1980	Exercises, Operations & Visits in European Waters
1 Feb 77-1 Jun 78	On Loan to FPS (Two successful arrests)
6 Jul 80-29 Mar 82	Extended Long Refit and Trials at Gibraltar
24 May 82	Recommissioned at Rosyth for 1st MCMS

1982-93	Exercises, Operations & Visits in European Waters
1 Jan 84	Transferred to newly formed 3rd MCMS based Rosyth
Jun 91-Sep 93	On loan to Fishery Protection Squadron

Significant Events:

9 Oct 62	Collision with BOSSINGTON during manoeuvres
May 66	Fired on by Indonesian shore batteries in Singapore Straits
4 Apr-4 Jul 75	Deployed to Port Said for Op RHEOSTAT TWO
Jul 78	Deep Armed Team Sweep Trials at Gibraltar
Aug-Sep 79	1st MCMS Deployment to Western Mediterranean
11 Jun 80	Collision with LEWISTON during Team Sweep
19 Apr-5 Jun 84	3rd MCMS Deployment to Mediterranean (inc Corfu)
23 May -4 Jul 86	3rd MCMS Deployment to Western Mediterranean
Aug-Dec 1988	Attached to STANAVFORCHAN
9 Oct-8 Nov 89	3rd MCMS Deployment to Western Mediterranean
21 Sep 93	Final Ton departure from Rosyth, with BRINTON

Paid Off: 5 Oct 93

Disposal: January 1998 to Pounds of Portsmouth, for break up.

Laid Down:	17th March 1953
Built by:	Montrose Shipbuilding Co Ltd
Completed:	16th November 1955
Time to Build:	32 months
Commissioned:	10th May 1957 for 51st (Trials) Minesweeping Squadron (MSS) based at Portland
Conversion:	to Minehunting Trials Ship 1956-57
Years Fully Operational:	20

Outline of Operational Career:

1957-1959	Initial Minehunting Equipment Trials
Aug 59-Jun 60	Deployment to USA and Canada for Minehunting System Evaluation Trials & Demonstrations
1961-62	Exercises in Home Waters and Minehunting System Demonstrations to European Navies.
1 Oct 62	1st Minehunting Squadron as SO based Port Edgar
1963-66	Minehunting Trials and Exercises in European Waters
1966-67	Conversion to Pump Jet Propulsion
5 Apr 67	Recommissioned for Trials of New Equipment as Senior Officer 3rd MCMS based Portland
1968-1978	Trials in UK Waters and European Port Visits including 58 Days Grenada Patrol 1973-77

Significant Events:

17 Oct 62	Attended Fleet Review by King Olaf of Norway
Jun-Jul 63	Operation CABLEWAY off Borkum
May 1964	Located wreck of Dutch ship 'De Liefede' sunk 1711
Mar-Aug 68	Search for Air Lingus Viscount a/c. 94 days on task
Jan 72	First PAP Trials (automated mini submarine) based in Brest

Paid Off:	23rd November 1978
Disposal:	2nd February 1981 Sold to CK Booth at Blyth for break up

Laid Down:	11th March 1955
Built by:	Fleetlands Shipyards Ltd (Gosport)
Completed:	17th September 1957
Time to Build:	30 months
Commissioned:	12th February 1958 for Fishery Protection Squadron (FPS) based Port Edgar
Years Fully Operational:	32

Outline of Operational Career:

24 Feb 58	Started first Fishery Protection patrol
1958-1992	Fishery Protection Patrols and Exercises in UK Waters
24 Jul 60	Visit of FPS to Grimsby for Freedom of Port Ceremony
May 63	Clearance Operation 'CLEAR ROAD' off Esjberg.
3 Jul 78	Started Long Refit at Chatham
14 Dec 79	Recommissioned for FPS at Chatham
7 Feb 92	Final Day of Fishery Patrol

Significant Events:

26 Apr 62	Fought fire in MV 'Olympic Thunder'. Salvage claim.
4 Sep 64	At opening of Forth Road Bridge by HM The Queen
6 Jan 67	Collision with LETTERSTON. Damage starboard side.

31 Mar 67	Took part in Oil Slick mop-up ex TORREY CANYON
1971	Carried out 16 successful FV arrests during year.
27 May 77	Salvaged French FV 'St Lucien' off Guernsey
12 Apr 82	Ships company manned NORTHELLA for Falklands War - continued Fishery Patrols with largely new crew.
8 May 84	At Opening of Thames Barrier by HM The Queen
8 Jul 87	Boarding Party locked down in Dutch FV Hold
28 Oct 89	Salvage of MV 'Fair Play- off Eddystone
30 Nov 90	Awarded Wilkinson Sword of Peace for 1990.
1992-97	SOBERTON employed as HQ for Woolwich Sea Cadets berthed off Erith

Paid Off: 1st March 1992

Disposal: 15th July 1998 Sold to Bakkerzonen at Bruges for Break-up

HMS STUBBINGTON Pennant No. M1204

Laid Down:	15th March 1954
Built by:	Camper & Nicholson Ltd, Gosport
Completed:	28th August 1956
Time to Build:	29 months
Commissioned:	2nd December 1957 for 108th Minesweeping Squadron (MSS) based Malta
Years Fully Operational:	25

Outline of Operational Career:

9-18 Dec 57	Passage to Malta
1958	3 Cyprus Patrols (95 days)
1959	4 Cyprus Patrols (132 days)
1960	2 refits in Malta totalling 8 months
1961-68	Exercises and Visits in Mediterranean
4 Sep –14 Dec 61	Deployment through Suez Canal to Aden and Karachi
20 Jan 69	Paid off for refit at Gibraltar, then passage to UK
16 Aug 69	Commissioned at VERNON as Sea Training CMS
1969-Jun 71	Training, Exercises and Visits in N. European Waters
26 Nov 71	Paid off for refit at Rosyth, then for 10th MCMS
26 Jun 72	Transferred to Tay Division RNR as HMS MONTROSE
Jun 72 -1975	RNR Sea Training, Exercises and Visits
18 Jan 76	Paid off at Chatham for 18 month refit
18 Jun 77	Commissioned at Chatham for FPS based Rosyth
1977-86	Fishery Protection Patrols in Home Waters

Significant Events:

5-12 Jun 67	Six Day War between Israel and Egypt
16-21 Jan 68	Disaster Relief after Western Sicilian Earthquake
13 Aug 80	Salvaged MV 'Mark' off Isle of Man
7 Sep 83	Salvaged FV 'Coronella' off Duncansby Head

Paid Off: 30th July 1986

Disposal: 26th September 1989 Sold for break-up in Bilbao, Spain

HMS SULLINGTON

Laid Down:	13th July 1953
Built by:	J S Doig (Grimsby) Ltd
Completed:	23rd March 1955
Time to Build:	22 Months
Commissioned:	23rd May 1955 for 50th (Trials) Minesweeping Squadron (MSS) based Portland
Years Fully Operational:	2 (as Minesweeper)

Outline of Operational Career:

27 May 55	Joined 50th MSS at Portland
1955	Hydrophone trials
1956	Hydrophone and Explosive Trials
1957-64	Conversion to Survey Vessel
17 Jul 64	Recommissioned as HMS MERMAID

Paid Off:	26th July 1957 (as CMS)
Disposal:	June 1971 Break Up by Kingston Vickers at Fleetwood

HMS TARLTON   Pennant No. M1186

Laid Down: 31st December 1953

Built by: J S Doig (Grimsby) Ltd

Completed: 14th December 1955

Time to Build: 24 months

Commissioned: 8th March 1956 for 108th Minesweeping Squadron (MSS) based Malta

Years Fully Operational: 4 months

Outline of Operational Career:

14-24 Mar 56	Passage to Malta to join 108th MSS
1 May-14 Jun 56	First (and only) Cyprus Patrol (42 days)
30 Jun-11 Jul 56	Passage to UK. To Reserve

Significant Events:

21-23 Mar 56	Met severe gale (Force 9, gusting 11) off Cape Bon. Sheltered Tunis Bay.

Paid Off: July 1956

Disposal: 1967 Sold to Argentina as 'RIO NEGRO'.

HMS THANKERTON

Pennant No. M1172

Laid Down:	16th March 1955
Built by:	Camper & Nicholson Ltd, Southampton
Completed:	10th May 1957
Time to Build:	26 months
Commissioned:	31st July 1957 for 108th Minesweeping Squadron MSS) based Malta
Years Fully Operational:	4 (RN)

Outline of Operational Career:

12 –23 Aug 57	Passage to Malta
1 Oct –18 Nov 47	First Cyprus Patrol (47 days)
19 Dec 57-19 Jan 58	Second Cyprus Patrol (31 days)
26 Feb-5 Mar 58	Third Cyprus Patrol (34 days)
13-21 May 58	Fourth Cyprus Patrol (9 days)
6-26 Jun 58	Fifth Cyprus Patrol (20 days)
30 Sep-14 Nov 58	Deployment to Aqaba, Aden and Berbera
1 Jan-4 Feb 59	Sixth Cyprus Patrol (35 days)
11 Apr-15 Apr 59	Seventh Cyprus Patrol (35 days)
30 May 59	Paid off to Reserve at Malta
18 Nov 59	Commissioned for passage to Singapore
8 Dec 59-19 Jan 60	Passage to Singapore
1 Feb 60	Paid off to reserve at Singapore
1960-64	Reserve Fleet Singapore
20 Jan 65	Commissioned at Singapore for 11th MSS
1965	Local Patrols off Singapore
Paid Off:	December 1965
Disposal:	8th April 1966 Sold to Royal Malaysian Navy as BRINCHANG

Laid Down:	1st May 1955
Built by:	J I Thorneycroft & Co, Southampton
Completed:	25th July 1956
Time to Build:	15 months
Commissioned:	August 1956 for 105th Minesweeping Squadron (MSS) based Harwich
Years Fully Operational:	33

Outline of Operational Career:

16 Aug 56	Joined 105th MSS at Harwich
23 Aug 7 Sep 56	Escorted Inshore Minesweepers to Malta
31 Oct-12 Nov 56	Operation MUSKETEER
7-17 Dec 56	Passage to UK. Paid off to reserve on arrival.
8 Nov 57	Commissioned for 100th MSS based VERNON
15-26 Sep 58	Passage to Malta with 100th MSS for Cyprus.
1-11 Dec 58	Passage to UK
1959	Exercises and Visits in N. European Waters
1 Jun 59	100th MSS transferred from VERNON to Port Edgar
20 Feb 65	2nd MSS Paid Off at Port Edgar to man 11th MSS ships at Singapore for Confrontation
3 Sep 65	Commissioned for 5th MSS based VERNON

5 Jan 66	Transferred to new 1st MCMS based Port Edgar
18 Feb 72	Transferred to new 2nd MCMS based VERNON
5 Sep 73	Rejoined 1st MCMS based Port Edgar
Jan-Apr 74	Attached to STANAVFORCHAN
27 Feb 75	Transferred to FPS based Port Edgar
19 Sep 75	Transferred to 10th MCMS
10 Apr 76-21 Mar 77	Extended Refit at Gibraltar.
22 Apr 77	Joined SW Group of 10th MCMS based Bristol
5 Nov 78	Transferred to NE Group 10th MCMS based Dundee
20 Aug 80	Transferred to 1st MCMS based Rosyth
1 Jan 84	Transferred to new 3rd MCMS based Rosyth
30 Mar 84	Transferred to FPS based Rosyth
1984-90	Fishery Protection Patrols in UK waters

Significant Events:

5-6 Nov 56	Took part in Operation MUSKETEER - Wire sweeping Group
13–16 Nov 56	Both Main Engines failed. Towed Port Said to Malta.
1-30 May 68	Took part in Op 'NEW BROOM' based Den Helder.
Oct-Dec 68 &70	Took part in 'Meet the Navy' cruises round UK
Sep 69	Assisted shipping in Gothenburg during severe gale.
30 Jun 75	Assisted in fighting fire in FV 'Bracoudene'
24 Jun 77	Attended Jubilee Review at Spithead
1981	Carried out 7 GRENADA Patrols (84 days) in year
Apr-Aug 1982	Crew manned HMS CORDELLA in South Atlantic
4 & 5 Dec 88	Assisted MV 'Bowsprit'. 4 C-in-C Commendations
Jul-Nov 89	7 successful arrests of foreign FV for infringements

Paid Off: 21st September 1990

Disposal: 21st October 1991 Sold to Brugse Scheepssloperij for break-up.

HMS WALKERTON

Laid Down:	4th July 1955
Built by:	J I Thornycroft, Southampton
Completed:	10th January 1958
Time to Build:	30 months
Commissioned:	24th February 1958 as Senior Officer 104th Minesweeping Squadron (MSS) based Malta
Years Fully Operational:	26

Outline of Operational Career:

3-27 Mar 58	Passage to Malta. Joined 104th MSS as SO
30 Apr –11 Jun 58	First Cyprus Patrol (40 days)
13 Aug to 8 Oct 58	Deployment to Aqaba and Aden
19 Dec 58-27 Jan 58	Second Cyprus Patrol (40 days)
20 Apr-23 May 59	Third Cyprus Patrol (34 days)
1-21 Aug 59	Fourth Cyprus Patrol (22 days)
6-13 Oct 59	Fifth Cyprus Patrol (8 days), then both engines unserviceable.
Oct 59	Transferred to 108th MSS as SO
2 Nov-3 Dec 59	Sixth Cyprus Patrol (31 days)
1960	Exercises and Visits in Mediterranean
3 Jul-1 Sep 61	Deployment to Aden, Bahrain and Kuwait
1 Oct 62	108th MSS renumbered 7th MSS
28 May–15 Jun 67	Deployed to Cyprus during Six Day War
31 Mar 69	7th MCMS left Malta. Last RN ships to leave.
4 Apr 69	Paid off to Reserve at Gibraltar
1 Jul 70	Commissioned Devonport as Dartmouth Training Ship
1970-79	Day running from Dartmouth for BRNC training

26 Jun 77	Attended Silver Jubilee Review at Spithead
27 Mar 79	Transferred to RNR Squadron, North West Group
11 Jun 79-3 Oct 80	Major Refit at Rosyth
11 Oct 80	Commissioned at Rosyth for FP Squadron

Significant Events:

28-29 Jan 59	Encountered severe gale north of Crete. 50° Roll. Both Main Engines out of action on arrival at Malta
26 Apr 60	Escorted HRH Prince Philip during visit to Malta
22-27 Jul 61	First visit of Ton Class to Bahrain (Later 9th MSS base)
26 Aug 61	Hit huge shark in Red Sea – underwater damage.
16-20 Jan 68	Rendered assistance after earthquake in W. Sicily
11 Nov 80	Collision with BRERETON during RAS -Stern damage
17 Dec 81	Collision with LEEDS CASTLE. Damage to bow.
13 Apr 82	Salvage of French FV 'Le Croise' off Isle of Man
24 Nov 83	Salvage of German MV 'Jans Peter' off Humber

Paid Off:	11th July 1985
Disposal:	20th December 1990. Sold to Ogdens of Middlesbrough for break-up

HMS WASPERTON   Pennant No. M1189/P1189

Laid Down:	21st June 1954
Built by:	White's Shipyard Ltd, Southampton
Completed:	19th July 1957
Time to Build:	37 months
Commissioned:	10th April 1958 for Fishery Protection Squadron (FPS) based Port Edgar
Years Fully Operational:	25 years
Conversion:	to Patrol Craft at Hong Kong 12th June to 7th September 1972

Outline of Operational Career:

30 Apr 58	Joined Fishery Protection Squadron at Port Edgar
1958 1971	Fishery Patrols, M/S Exercises and Port Visits
12 Jan-28 Apr 72	Passage to Hong Kong round Africa
28 Apr 72	Joined 6th Patrol Craft Squadron based Hong Kong
1972-1984	Local Patrols, Exercises & Visits in South China Sea
1 Jun 73	6th PCS renamed Hong Kong Squadron

Significant Events:

26 Sep 61	Visited St Kilda with GOC Scotland embarked
1967	5 Successful arrests for Fishery infringements
1968	4 Successful arrests for Fishery Infringements

Paid Off:	19th November 1984
Disposal:	1985 Sold to Pounds of Portsmouth for local disposal in Hong Kong

HMS WILKIESTON Pennant No. M1192

Laid Down:	1st July 1955
Built by:	Cook, Welton & Gemmell Ltd, Beverley, Yorkshire
Completed:	24th July 1957
Time to Build:	25 months
Commissioned:	15th December 1957 at Hythe for 104th MSS based at Malta
Years Fully Operational:	12 years

Outline of Operational Career:

19-28 Jan 58	Passage to Malta to join 104th MSS
May-Aug 58	3 periods of Cyprus Patrol (Total 45 days)
9 Aug-31 Oct 58	Deployment to Aden & Aqaba via Suez Canal
Jan-Aug 59	3 periods of Cyprus Patrol (Total 116 days)
21 Oct-30 Nov 59	Passage to Singapore with 104th MSS
1960-1962	Exercises and Port Visits in South China Sea
1 Oct 62	104th MSS renumbered 6th MSS
13 Dec 62-2 Jan 63	1st period of N. Borneo Patrol (20 days)
1963	7 periods of North Borneo Patrol (Total 129 days)
1964	5 Periods of North Borneo Patrol (Total 145 days)
1965	7 periods of North Borneo Patrol (Total 84 days): 10 periods of Singapore Straits Patrol (126 days)
1966	2 periods of North Borneo Patrol (Total 35 days) 4 periods Singapore Straits Patrol (31 days)
1967-1968	Exercises and Port Visits in South China Sea
14 Jan 67	Transferred to 8th MCMS as SO, based Hong Kong
5 Oct 67	Transferred back to 6th MCMS.
5 Jul-15 Dec 69	Passage to UK eastabout via Pacific/Atlantic

Significant Events:

2 Feb 60	Rescued crew of MV 'Coral Sea' (USA) with FISKERTON
10-17 May 62	Anti-piracy patrol off Borneo with BULWARK
Sep 67	Collision with WOOLASTON during manoeuvres
Jul-Dec 69	Passage to UK with HOUGHTON (SO) via Darwin, South Pacific Islands, Hawaii, California, Mexico, Panama Canal, Jamaica & Bermuda.

Paid Off: December 1969

Disposal: September 1976 Sold to Whites of St Davids for break up.

HMS WILTON   Pennant No. M1116

Laid Down: 7th August 1970

Built by: Vosper Thornycroft, Southampton

Completed: 12th June 1973

Time to Build: 34 months World's first GRP hull warship

Commissioned: 14th July 1973 for 2nd Minecountermeasures Squadron (MCMS) based Portsmouth

Years Fully Operational: 21 years

Outline of Operational Career:

20 Mar-20 Nov 74	Deployed to Port Said for Operation RHEOSTAT
1975-1883	Exercises, Route Survey & Visits in N. Europe
3 Jan-19 June 77	Attached to STANAVFORCHAN
17 May-31 Dec 79	Attached to STANAVFORCHAN as Senior Officer
10 Jan 1980	Rejoined 2nd MCMS
28 Mar-5 Nov 84	Deployed to Mediterranean. Visits & Exercises inc:
29 Aug-4 Oct 84	Operation HARLING – Mine Clearance Gulf of Suez
14 Sep 87-Jun 88	Temporary transfer to Fishery Protection Squadron

16 Jun 88	Joined 3rd MCM Squadron based at Portsmouth
21 May 91-Jul 94	To BRNC Dartmouth as Navigation Training Ship

Significant Events:

7 Apr-1 Nov 74	Suez Canal for Operation RHEOSTAT
1976	7 Periods of Op GRENADA off Northern Ireland
28 Jun 77	Took part in Silver Jubilee Review at Spithead
31 Aug 79	Collided with BNS BREYDEL off Ostende

Paid Off: July 1994

Disposal: Sold to TAE Marine in October 2000, then resold in October 2001 as Essex Sailing Club HQ

Laid Down:	20th January 1956
Built by:	Wivenhoe Shipyard
Completed:	17th February 1960
Time to Build:	49 months
Commissioned:	8th April 1960 for 100th Minesweeping Squadron (MSS) based at Rosyth
Years Fully Operational:	15

Outline of Operational Career:

1 May 60	Joined 100th MSS at Rosyth
1960-64	Exercises and Visits in North European Waters
1 Oct 62	100th MSS renamed 2nd MSS
Jan 65	Paid off at Rosyth. Crew to man Ton in Far East
15 Sep 65	Recommissioned at Rosyth as SO 1st MCMS
31 Mar 66	Paid off at Devonport. Crew to WOLVERTON
Oct-Dec 66	Passage to Persian Gulf round Africa
Dec 66	Joined 9th MCMS based Bahrain as SO
1967-71	Exercises, Patrols and Visits in Gulf Area.
5 Sep-13 Nov 71	Passage to UK round Africa
Jan 72	Allocated to Tyne Div RNR as NORTHUMBRIA
1 Jan 72-31 Dec 75	10th MCMS based Newcastle. Training Periods
1 Jan 76	Allocated NE Group. Name reverted to WISTON

Significant Events:

11-30 May 63	Took part in Op 'CLEAR ROAD' based Esjberg
9-26 Oct 63	Took part in Op 'ICE SCOT' based Iceland
20 Sep 76	Present at collision of HMS FITTLETON with HMS MERMAID in Channel. Assisted in recovery phase
28 Jun 76	Present at Spithead Review

Paid Off:	October 1977
Disposal:	9th August 1982 Sold to Kitson Vickers, Whitby for break-up

Laid Down:	28th September 1954
Built by:	Montrose Shipyard
Completed:	25th March 1958
Time to Build:	42 months
Commissioned:	5th September 1958 for 100th Minesweeping Squadron (MSS) based Portsmouth
Years Fully Operational:	26 years
Conversion:	to Patrol Craft in Rosyth Dockyard 29th August to 24th November 1971

Outline of Operational Career:

16-26 Sep 58	Deployment to Malta for Cyprus Patrol
9 Oct-28 Nov 58	First (and only) Cyprus Patrol
1-11 Dec 58	Passage to UK
1959 -1964	Exercises and Visits in North European Waters
2 Mar-4 Apr 60	Deployment to Malta for Exercises
1 Oct 62	100th MSS renamed 2nd MSS
9 Oct 64	Paid off Port Edgar. Crew to man Ton in Far East
9 Jun 65	Recommissioned for 5th MSS based VERNON
13 May 66	Transferred to 1st MCMS based Port Edgar
1966 -1971	Exercises, Trials and Visits in European Waters
29 Aug-24 Nov 71	Conversion to Patrol Craft in Rosyth Dockyard
12 Jan-28 Apr 72	Passage to Hong Kong Round Africa for 6th PCS
1972-1984	Local Patrols, Exercises & Visits in South China Sea
1 Jun 73	6th PCS renamed Hong Kong Dragon Squadron

Significant Events:

13-28 May 1963	Took part in Op 'CLEAR ROAD' based Esjberg
17 Jun-10 Jul 63	Took part in Op 'CABLEWAY' based Den Helder
16-22 Sep 63	Took part in Op 'ICE SCOT' based Iceland
1-30 May 68	Took part in Op ' NEW BROOM' based Den Helder
27 Jun–14 Nov 69	Took part in 'Meet the Navy' Visits to UK Ports
4 May 75	Present for HM The Queen's Visit to HMS TAMAR
15 May-6 Jun 81	Visits to South Korea and Japan
6 Mar 83	Grounded in Hong Kong Harbour. Propellor damage

Paid Off: September 1984 for local sale and conversion for 'further use'

Laid Down:	27th August 1954
Built by:	Herd & MacKenzie Ltd, Buckie
Completed:	10th October 1958
Time to Build:	49 months
Commissioned:	4th December 1958 for 104th Minesweeping Squadron (MSS) based Malta
Years Fully Operational:	15

Outline of Operational Career:

14-24 Dec 58	Passage to Malta. Joined 104th MSS
Apr 59	First (and only) Cyprus Patrol
6 Nov –14 Dec 59	Passage from Malta to Singapore with MARYTON
1960-62	Exercises and Visits in South China Sea
20-27 Feb 62	First anti-piracy patrol off Taiwau, Borneo
5-10 Apr 62	Escorted Inshore MSS Hong Kong to Singapore
Sep 62-Jan 63	2 North Borneo Patrols (48 days)
1963	5 periods of North Borneo Patrol (128 days)
1964	6 periods of North Borneo Patrol (138 days)One period of Singapore Straits Patrol (11 days)
1965	5 Periods of North Borneo Patrol (71 days)13 Periods of Singapore Straits Patrol (127 days)
1966	One period of North Borneo Patrol (22 days)
25 Jan 67	Transferred to 8th MCMS based Hong Kong
5 Oct 67	8th MCMS disbanded. Reverted to 6th MCMS
29 Jan-17 Apr 68	Passage to Gibraltar round Africa with FISKERTON
18 Apr 68	Paid off at Gibraltar for Long Refit

29 Apr 69	Commissioned for 10th MCMS as THAMES
1969-71	Training periods & 10th MCMS exercises at Gibraltar
1972-75	RNR training periods & visits based Southampton

Significant Events:

Jun 58	Located UAR Landing Craft adrift south of Cyprus and towed it to Limassol
24 Oct-10 Nov 60	Visits to Burmese ports with 104th MSS
25 Jun 65	Booby-trapped sampan exploded alongside in Singapore Straits, killing Midshipman Michael Finch
April-May 66	Suffered underwater damage from submerged log while on patrol. 11 weeks in Singapore Dockyard on return.

Paid Off: 10th November 1975

Disposal: 14th November 1980 Sold to Liguria Maritime, Sittingbourne – break-up.

Laid Down:	25th June 1954
Built by:	Philip & Son, Dartmouth
Completed:	13 June 1957
Time to Build:	36 months
Commissioned:	18th April 1958 for Fishery Protection Squadron (FPS) based Port Edgar
Years Fully Operational:	25

Outline of Operational Career:

May 1958	Joined Fishery Protection Squadron at Port Edgar
1958-1971	UK Fishery Patrols, Exercises and Visits
1 Nov 67	Fishery Protection Squadron became 4th MCMS
1-16 Oct 68	Took part in trials of Hovercraft in FP Role
1 Nov 71	Transferred to 3rd MCMS based Portland
1973	Carried out 4 periods of Grenada Patrol (25 days)
12 Jul-9 Aug 75	Deep Armed Team Sweep Trials off Gibraltar
1975	Carried out 5 periods of Grenada Patrol (42 days)
17 Jul–19 Aug 76	Deep Armed Team Sweep Trials off Gibraltar
1976	Carried out 3 periods of Grenada Patrol (23 days)
20 Feb 77-7 Apr 78	Long Refit at Gibraltar
31 May 78	Joined Fishery Protection Squadron at Rosyth
1979-84	UK Fishery Patrols, Exercises and Visits
12-24 Oct 80	Temporary attachment to STANAVFORCHAN
14 Apr 82	Majority of WOTTON's crew transferred to FARNELLA for service in the Falklands
1 Apr 84	Transferred to 10th (RNR) MCMS for London Div
21 Apr-20 May 84	Deployment to Gibraltar: NATO & RNR Exercises

Significant Events:

1966	Made 4 successful FV arrests in UK waters
28 Apr-26 May 68	Took part in Operation NEW BROOM 68
Jul-Oct 68	Made 4 successful FV arrests in UK waters
12-14 Dec 69	Experienced Violent Storm Force 11 in Shetlands
6 –7 Jun 1973	Salvaged FV 'Tina Louise' off Portland.
2 Jul 78	Stood by FV 'Storgen' on fire off May Island.
6 Mar 84	Firefighting in MV 'Anna Tholstrup' in Irish Sea

Paid Off: November 1984

Disposal: Loaned to Woolwich Unit, Sea Cadets 1986-89
19th November 1992 – Sold to Brugse Scheepssloperij for break-up

HMS YARNTON Pennant No. M1196

Laid Down:	21st October 1954
Built by:	William Pickersgill & Sons, Sunderland
Completed:	16th January 1957
Time to Build:	27 months
Commissioned:	11th May 1957 for 100th Minesweeping Squadron (MSS) based Portsmouth
Conversion:	to Patrol Craft at Hong Kong July to December 1973 (Part Conversion in Oct-Nov 71)
Years Fully Operational:	26

Outline of Operational Career:

Jun 57	Joined 100th MSS
1-12 Sep 58	100th MSS deployed to Malta for Cyprus Patrols
18 Sep-25 Nov 58	First (and only) Cyprus Patrol
1-11 Dec 58	100th MSS returned to Portsmouth
1959-1964	Exercises and Visits in North European Waters
10 Jun 59	100th MSS transferred base to Port Edgar
1 Oct 62	100th MSS renumbered 2nd MSS
18 Jan 65	2nd MSS paid off to man 11th MSS at Singapore
Aug 65	Recommissioned at Port Edgar for 2nd MSS
Jan-Oct 66	Long Refit at Chatham
17 Oct 66	Sailed from UK to join 9th MCMS at Bahrain
16 Nov 66	Arrived Bahrain. 4 months repairs post cyclone.
1967 -1971	Patrols, Exercises and Visits in Gulf/Indian Ocean
3 Jun-19 Sep 67	Deployments to Aden during and after 6 Day War
22 Jul-23 Dec 68	Deployment to Singapore for refit
1 Oct 70–29 Apr 71	Deployment to Singapore for refit

14 Aug 71	9th MCMS disbanded. YARNTON to Hong Kong
17 Sep 71	Joined 6th Patrol Craft Squadron at Hong Kong
1972-84	Local patrols, exercises and visits in S E Asia.

Significant Events:

9-30 May 63	Took part in Op CLEAR ROAD based Esjberg
17 Jun-11 Jul 63	Took part in Op CABLE WAY based Den Helder
9-26 Sep 63	Took part in Op ICE SCOTT based Iceland
16-25 Apr 64	Took part in Op CLEAR ROAD 2 based Den Helder
9-10 Nov 66	Encountered cyclone in Arabian Sea. Bad damage.
16-27 Jan 70	Dhofar Coast Patrol during insurgency
9 Jan 72	Assisted QUEEN ELIZABETH 1 fire at Hong Kong
31 Jul 77	H K Squadron awarded Wilkinson Sword of Peace

Paid Off: 12th November 1984

Disposal: 1986. Sold to Pounds of Portsmouth for local disposal in Hong Kong

TONs that served in Other Navies

HMS		Service & Dates
	Argentina – 6	
Bevington	Tierra del Fuego	1967 - ?
Hickelton	Neuquen	1967 - ?
Ilmington	Formosa	1967 - 2003 Broken up 2005
Rennington #	Chaco	Last unmodified TONs in active service in any navy
Santon	Chabut	1967 - ?
Tarlton	Rio Negro	1967 - ?
	Australia – 6	All served in Confrontation 1964-66
Alcaston	Snipe	8/62 – 6/83. Broken up 1985
Chediston	Curlew	9/62 – 4/90 Sold for private use reported to be in Tasmania
Jackton #	Teal	8/62 – 7/75 Still active off Cyprus as private diving vessel
Singleton #	Ibis	9/62 – 5/84. Broken up 1984
Somerleyton #	Hawk	7/62 – 1/72. Broken up 1977
Swanston #	Gull	10/62 – 11/69. Broken up 1987
	Ghana – 1	
Aldington	Ejura	Loaned 1964, Purchased 1974, Decommissioned 1981
	India – 4	
Durweston #	Kakinda	
Wennington #	Cuddalore	1956 – 1981 formed 149th MSS
Whitton #	Cannamore	
Overton #	Karwar	
	Ireland – 3	
Alverton	Banba	
Blaxton	Fola	1971 – 1986
Oulston #	Grainne	
	Malaysia – 7	All served in Confrontation 1963-66. As 25th MSS
Darlaston	Mahamiru	1960 – 80/82
Dilston	Jerai	1964 – 80/82
Edderton	Perantau	1969 – 82.
Essington	Kinabalu	1964 – 80/82
Hexton	Ledang	1963 – 80/82
Lullington	Tahan	1/66 – 80/82
Thankerton	Brinchang	4/66 – 80/82
	New Zealand – 2	
Hickleton		4/64 – 12/66 Loaned to RNZN for Confrontation.
Santon		Both transferred to Argentina in 1967
	South Africa – 10	
Castleton #	Johannesburg	6/59 – 1985. Broken up 1989
Chilton #	East London	10/58 – 1989. 2003 sold for film props then broken up
Dumbleton #	Port Elizabeth	10/58 – 1985. Broken up 1989
Dunkerton #	Pretoria	8/55 – 12/87 Sold as museum exhibit. 1998 re-built as yacht, then active as Madiba, underwater survey vessel. Reverted to Golden Firefly and up for auction Aug 2010
Hazleton #	Kaapstad	8/55 – 1985. Broken up 1989
Oakington #	Mosselbaai	9/59 – 12/85. Broken up 1989
Packington #	Walvisbaai	9/59 – 9/01. Sold for filming 2003. Rebuilt 2012 yacht MOJO.
Stratton #	Kimberley	6/59 – 1989. Broken up 2003
Built in UK	Windhoek	4/58 – 1989. Broken up 2003
for SAN	Durban	4/58 – Preserved as museum ship in Durban

Never commissioned for RN Service. Put into reserve on completion of building & later transferred.

Operational Analysis

Certain aspects of the historical perspective of the TON Class make for embarrassing reading.

At a construction cost of approximately £252,000 for each of the 117 wooden-hulled TONs, it has to be asked if the UK taxpayer received full value on the investment of about £29.5 million.

Years of Operational Service in RN						
	< 1	< 5	6-10	11-20	21-30	>30
Ships	5	21	14	24	27	6

Average time to build was 28.6 months and average length of service in the RN was 14 years.

Most ship owners, be that of merchant ship, pleasure yacht or even warship, would expect to obtain a return of more than twenty years of service from their vessels, but only 28% of the 98 TONS which served in the RN achieved that.

Minimum periods of service were HEXTON (3 months) and TARLETON (4 months) before they were transferred to the Malaysian and Argentinean Navies respectively.

A further 18 vessels never saw RN service but were placed in reserve on completion of building and subsequently transferred to other navies.

The longest serving vessels were: BICKINGTON 32 years, BRERETON 33 years, BRONINGTON 31 years, NURTON 36 years, SHERATON 33 years and UPTON 33 years.

Part of the reason for the short service of many others was the policy of placing the ships in strategic reserve at sensitive points in the UK, Mediterranean, Aden and Singapore, where they could be activated at relatively short notice and brought to an operational condition within a few weeks, given availability of trained manpower and suitable dockyard support.

The effectiveness of this strategy was tested from time to time, as ships rotated from arked condition for service with the Royal Naval Reserve and during Confrontation.

The strategic planners may however, have paid insufficient attention to the problem of the marine worm, to counter which Nelson's navy adopted copper bottoming. Wooden hulls left swinging round a buoy in warm tropical waters deteriorated at an alarming rate and many of these were written off as "beyond economical repair" within a dozen years of their launch.

The computation of how many personnel [aka sailors] served in TONs is much more complicated than just multiplying an average ships company of 35 x two year commission x 14 years average service per ship x 98 RN ships [c. 24,000]. Manning levels varied with role and area of deployment. Every time the RNR put to sea they invariably carried ten more personnel than designed, as everyone wanted a crack at sea time and, typically, they maintained three operational crews for each ship. Ships trialling equipment usually carried additional personnel; base staff and civilian scientists and several ships swapped ships companies to meet operational needs. A conservative estimate suggests that over the 40 year history of the TONs more than 35,000 officers and ratings served in them and many a future admiral had his first experience of a sea-going command in a TON.

Despite some of the gloomy statistics listed above, the nation certainly achieved its monies' worth in terms of the development of specialist skills and experience in a significant proportion of the Navy's manpower, often in situations of physical danger and sometimes in the face of a hostile opponent. Plus, excellent PR as TONs regularly showed the flag, at home and abroad, in ports not visited by bigger ships.

Cover theme for "Last of the Wooden Walls"

HMS ALFRISTON in heavy weather off Anvil Point, Dorset, 1980

Painted by Tony Hunt

ALFRISTON was manned by an RNR crew from HMS WESSEX, Southampton

Last of the Wooden Walls – a history of the TON Class

Last of the Wooden Walls – a history of the TON Class explains the concept of the non-magnetic coastal minesweeper, details of construction and capabilities, their machinery, armament and specialised equipment for minesweeping and mine hunting, the deployments of the various squadrons and the campaigns in which they engaged, together with details of support ships and establishments. The valuable contribution of the Royal Naval Reserve and details of the service of TONs in other navies, rounds off this enthralling narrative.

"Last of the Wooden Walls" and the companion "TON Ship Histories" together form a valuable work of reference for the naval historian and a jolly good adventure story for all who love the sea and ships.

Last of the Wooden Walls may be ordered from

**Halsgrove Publications Ltd,
Halsgrove House, Ryelands Industrial Estate, Bagley Road,
Wellington, Somerset, TA21 9PZ**

Tel: 01823 653777

e-mail: sales@halsgrove.com

Minesweeping is a science of vague assumptions,

based on debatable figures,

taken from inconclusive experiments,

performed with instruments of problematic accuracy,

by persons of doubtful reliability

and questionable mentality

Anonymous RNVR Officer - 1943